Frozen in Time

Frozen in Time

The Enduring Legacy of the 1961 U.S. Figure Skating Team

Nikki Nichols

For further information, contact the publisher at

Emmis Books
1700 Madison Road
Cincinnati, OH 45206
www.emmisbooks.com

Library of Congress Cataloging-in-Publication Data

Nichols, Nikki, 1975-
Frozen in time : the enduring legacy of the 1961 US figure skating team / by Nikki Nichols.
p. cm.
Includes index.
Includes bibliographical references.
ISBN-13: 978-1-57860-260-5
ISBN-10: 1-57860-260-2
1. Figure skating. 2. Figure skaters--United States--Biography. 3. Aircraft accidents--Belgium. I. Title.
GV850.4.N55 2006
796.91'2'0922--dc22

2005021563

On front cover and half title page, screened background image: Members of the U.S. Figure Skating Team pose before boarding Belgian Sabena Airline Plane at New York's Idlewild Airport Feb 14, 1961. Photo courtesy AP Images.

Distributed by Publishers Group West

Edited by Jack Heffron
Cover and interior designed by Andrea Kupper

Dedicated to the members of the 1961 U.S. Figure Skating Team, their coaches, the officials, and the loving family members who died in the crash of Sabena Flight 548, and to everyone who works to preserve their memory.

Special thanks to the USFSA for immense assistance in archival research and interview contacts, and a sincere thanks to everyone who took the time to share their stories for this tribute.

The biggest "thank you" of all to my parents, Michael and Catherine Nichols, who supported me throughout this endeavor in countless ways, and to my beloved fiancé, pairs partner, and friend, Michael J. Cunningham, who believes in me as a writer, skater, and person.

Acknowledgments

Special thanks to the United States Figure Skating Association and the World Figure Skating Museum and Hall of Fame for providing unfettered access to materials pertaining to the crash. Great thanks to my coach, Kim Seybold Catron, for inspiring my growing passion for skating. And a huge thanks to Ronald Ludington, who helped in countless ways.

Thanks to two talented writers, Charles Haas and Matthew Gladden, for their wonderful editing suggestions and moral support. Most of all, I offer my most profound thanks to Jack Heffron of Emmis Books for his editing acumen and great belief in this project.

Thanks to the following individuals for granting interviews and providing materials and support:

Roberto Agnolini
Dr. Tenley Albright
Randy Bairnsfather and the Town of Winchester Archives
Belgian Ministry of Communications
William Boeck
Jim Browning
Joyce Butchart and the Seattle Figure Skating Club
Diane Cassidy and the Cheyenne Mountain Heritage Center
Sven Christiansen
Dr. Lorraine Hanlon Comanor
Debbie Conrad
Michael J. Cunningham
Carol and William Cunningham
Howard Deardorff
Ann de Brabander
Annie and Diane de Leeuw
Kathi Doak
Susan Duncan
Jane Dystel
Charles Foster
Belinda Gillett
Diana Hall and the Ottawa Public Library

Ruth Harle
Dan Hollander
Eileen Seigh Honnen
Lee Hubby
Maria Jelinek
Tanya Howe Johnson
Jane Bucher Jones
U.S. Senator Edward M. Kennedy
Sally Knoll
Tonia Kwiatkowski
Sandy Lamb
Emery Leger
Mickey Leiter
Ron Ludington
Paul Maca
Sandy Masengale
Virginia Might
Melody Miller
Mark Mitchell
Catherine and Michael Nichols
John Nicks
Kevin O'Sullivan
Roberta Parkinson
Amy Partain
Pikes Peak Library
Barbara Ramsay
Yvette Reyes
Diane Yeomans Robins
Richard Rosborough
Elizabeth (Sherry) Ruch and the
Minto Figure Skating Club
Tom Schiebel
Allison Scott
Shelley Seyfried-Bourg
Skate Canada
Cathy Stevensen
Diana LeMaire Squibb
Bob Sullivan
United States Olympic Committee
Elizabeth Viken
Rose Anne Wager
Dixie Wilson
Peter Winters
Ben and Mary Louise Wright
Barbara Yeager
Beverly Yeomans
Pam and Gary Yohler

Foreword

Every time I lace a pair of figure skates and take to the ice, a corner of my heart aches for the skaters of the 1961 U.S. figure skating team. I silently pay homage, occasionally practicing the layback spin variation performed so enchantingly by 1961 champion Laurence Owen. Those skaters were stolen before their time—never again able to grace the frozen paradise they roamed in life—and never able to prove their mastery while the world watched.

As a skater, I know all too well what drew them to the sport. Skating can be a sanctuary. The wondrous feeling of flight, of gliding across the ice, strips away any stress or sorrow, any pain or pressure. For a figure skater, every ice rink possesses a seductive power, offering freedom from everything outside it. And there is pleasure in the rituals of skating: the precision of lacing a pair of boots to just the right tightness, paying no mind to the hardened blisters and calluses on the fingers; the first moment of contact with the ice, when the ears are more sensitive to the sound of the blades scraping the first lines on a freshly cut ice surface; the chilly wind hitting the face as more speed is generated. And then there is landing a jump perfectly on one foot, arms stretched out and chin up, as if to say, "Take that!"

The skaters you'll read about in these pages were the top finishers at the 1961 U.S. National Championships. Winning a medal at Nationals earned each skater passage aboard Sabena Flight 548, a state-of-the-art Boeing 707. The plane would take them to Brussels, where they planned to board a new plane for Prague, host city of the 1961 World Figure Skating Championships. Some of the skaters brought parents or older siblings as chaperones. Coaches and judges also boarded the plane, and some of them brought spouses and children. When the plane crashed in a Belgian field on February 15, 1961, entire families were shattered, and the American skating program suffered a staggering blow that threatened to cripple it for many years. That tragic event still resonates deeply with champion figure skaters today. Michelle Kwan, whose longtime coach, Frank Carroll, was coached by Maribel Vinson Owen, cited a "cosmic connection" to Maribel after winning her ninth U.S. national figure skating title in 2005. On that evening, Michelle tied Maribel for the highest number of women's titles in American figure skating history.

Frozen in Time takes you on a journey back in time to experience the highly competitive U.S. National and North American championships of that fateful year. The skaters performed in a different way and in a very different atmosphere than the one we know today. Beginning in 1960, television revolutionized the sport, bringing skaters to unforeseen levels of popularity and even changing the rules of competition. This story takes place in the final days of what now seems like an antique era, when the world was black and white, when figure skating was not a well-publicized sport. It also takes place on the cusp of a new era, when the skaters on that team would have become media stars whose names are as well known as the stars who followed them, such as Peggy Fleming.

I've done my best to provide a portrait, sometimes an intimate one, of the skaters' and coaches' lives—from their beginnings on the ice to the many painful sacrifices made to continue in their quest for gold. During the three years it took to research and write this book, I remained continually surprised that it had not been told before in any depth. It was an unprecedented moment in the history of American sport. On board the plane were some of the most revolutionary people figure skating has ever known. I often felt inadequate to the task of providing for such amazing people a fitting tribute. As I wrote, I also fell under the spell of two families of women—the Owens and the Westerfelds. This is very much the story of women—women ahead of their time, living independently, mothers and daughters and sisters with complex relationships that were demanding as well as nurturing, full of sacrifice and laughter and love.

In their lives, the people on board the plane were vivacious, talented, graceful champions. In death, they have become heroes to many who don't realize the impact their deaths continue to have on the sport. In these pages, I hope a new audience will gain an appreciation for their gifts—an audience that was robbed of the chance to see them pursue the Olympic dream.

Chapter One

Laurence Owen bounded through the hallways of the Broadmoor Ice Palace sporting a luminous grin as she shook the fresh coating of snow off her boots. Mother and sister in tow, she walked with a self-possession beyond her years. Her long-legged stride suggested a genuine confidence hard to find in girls of sixteen. Her mere presence brought pause to the host of rabidly busy people working to ready the venue for the 1961 U.S. National Figure Skating Championships.

They must have wondered in amazement, "What is she so happy about? Isn't she nervous?" Though only sixteen years old, Laurence seemed to absorb her surroundings with a sort of nostalgia about the history she was poised to make. She knew, too, that this was not simply a competition—but a *coronation*. In a country with only the fictional monarchies of beauty pageants and movie stars, in America there were, too, the "ice queens." They had all the qualities befitting true royalty. With their sparkling, brilliantly colorful costumes, they looked as regal and lovely as any fairy tale queen. They were graceful and strong under pressure, in a world where their every move was scrutinized. And their lives were as dramatic and heartbreaking as the lives of true royals. In 1961, the title of ice queen was vacant, and dozens of eager ice princesses readied themselves to leap, spin, and dance to obtain it.

While other competitors, keenly aware of the life-altering importance involved in such an event, paced the arena's halls in a perpetual state of panic and worry, Laurence, readily flashing her wide, joyous smile, was the picture of serenity. As she bounded along the hallways of the arena, her dark-brown hair cropped close to her face, she radiated an internal contentment. She was poised, sure, smiling, and relaxed. The bounce in her step didn't suggest arrogance, yet it appeared that she knew what others would soon find out. This was *her* year. She was going to make her peers at the Skating Club of Boston proud. She smiled as if she had already won, though the biggest test was still days away.

Competitors, rink employees, journalists, judges, officials, and parents overwrought with nerves crowded the halls, creating warmth in the usually cold ice rink, which had just been remodeled for the event. The smell of fresh paint hung in the air.

Some of the skaters prepared for their practice, the first opportunity to see if nerves remained under control, or if pre-competition jitters had transformed otherwise good legs into something with the consistency of Jell-O. While others walked the hallways or sat in the seats of the mostly empty arena, those getting ready to glide onto the ice stretched their legs, bending their knees, touching their toes, each seemingly oblivious of everyone around them. In the intimidating atmosphere competitors donned their most serious and focused facial expressions. They did not have time to socialize with each other on the ice, for every minute of practice was needed for the business of winning a championship.

Each practice session clicked by faster than most of the sweater-clad competitors would have liked. The superstitious types often felt that a poor practice signaled a good competition to come.

The more relaxed skaters felt that at this point it would be hard to improve upon what had already been toiled over hundreds, if not thousands, of times before.

As the growling Zamboni emerged through the wide swinging doors, most of the young men and women hurriedly tried to throw one more jump into the practice, believing that just one more time would help the moves snap into place—that one more successfully executed double loop or flying camel would spark the confidence they needed.

Some of the skaters left the ice grudgingly. Others were ready for a cold drink and a comfortable chair, but coaches, many of whom doubled as coach and parent, urged their prodigies to keep going even in the face of fatigue. As one practice session ended, the Colorado College hockey team, bright and blazing in their white, black, and gold uniforms, thundered onto the ice, nearly knocking several skaters off their blades and into a battered heap. Disaster was averted, but this interruption meant additional work would have to wait.

The usual gathering of newspaper reporters mingled with the competitors, coaches, and parents as well as with a new group of participants at the event—production and camera crews from CBS. For the first time in the history of the sport, the United States Figure Skating Championships would be shown on television. In living rooms across America, hundreds of thousands—maybe even millions—of viewers would take a front-row seat to watch every spin, landing, and fall. The event would be broadcast a few weeks later, unlike today, when the important figure skating events are usually broadcast live.

CBS television had aired the 1960 Winter Olympic Games from Squaw Valley, California, a year earlier to rave reviews. The most celebrated moment in those games occurred when a group of American college boys defeated the heavily favored hockey team from communist Russia. For those who lived through it, this team showed just as much grit as the 1980 "Miracle on Ice" team that beat the Soviets in the Lake Placid Winter Games semifinal. Though the U.S. hockey program had won the two previous Olympic silver medals, in the 1960 Games, these scrappy American amateurs were considered overwhelming underdogs to the Soviets, Czechs, and Canadians. Just as in 1980, the U.S. faced the Soviets in the semifinals. The U.S. beat them, the first time the Americans had ever beaten the Soviets in hockey. They went on to beat the Czechs for the gold. In the height of the simmering Cold War, these victories ignited a fire of enthusiasm in America.

Figure skating, in addition to hockey, captured many eyes and hearts in the 1960 Olympics. Carol Heiss, the movie-star-pretty American figure skater, took to the ice with a fierce athleticism, landing a double Axel and forever securing her legacy as a brilliant champion. She had already won a silver medal at the 1956 Olympic Games, and now Heiss had won the gold medal to complete her stellar collection. Newspapers of the day labeled her "Cinderella of the blades." Her triumph was part of only thirteen hours of Olympic competition shown on television—a stark contrast to today's wall-to-wall network and cable coverage.

Following the ratings success of the Winter Games, the television network decided to broadcast portions of the 1960 Summer Olympics. The Rome Games produced some of the most enduring champions in their respective fields—Wilma Rudolph in track and field, and the indomitable Cassius Clay in boxing.

Carol Heiss, Cassius Clay, Wilma Rudolph, and the USA hockey team created a spark that leapt right through television sets to captivate viewers. Suddenly, these athletes were the toast of America, even if tense race relations tempered this new social status for some of the black athletes. Television executives longed to capitalize on this new fascination with sport and its beautiful, fiery players. Their athletic gifts and human imperfections fascinated equally, and all facets of both the sport and the athlete seemed to make for dramatic television viewing.

The presence of television cameras at the Broadmoor Ice Palace added a new sizzle of excitement for the skaters, who must have sensed, at some level, that their sport, like many others, was entering a new phase of visibility. Television, as they knew, was influencing all areas of modern life. In the 1960 presidential election, John F. Kennedy famously wore makeup during the first-ever televised debate between presidential candidates. Richard Nixon did not powder his face, and Americans ended up choosing Kennedy as their president. No one can say with certainty that Kennedy won the election because of the new medium, but Kennedy himself credited TV with making a definite difference in the election returns. He said, "We wouldn't have had a prayer without that gadget." And so Camelot began.

FCC Chairman Newton Minnow did not share the new president's enthusiasm for the new medium, referring to it in a famous 1961 speech as "a vast wasteland." Regardless, in 1961, ninety percent of Americans owned television sets, and millions of sets of eyes were about to be treated to the first broadcast of a U.S. National Skating Championship.

CBS devoted Sunday afternoons to the new sports craze, in a show fittingly titled *CBS Sports Spectacular.* The anthology-style show began just thirteen weeks after the 1960 Summer Olympics and featured everything from the sublime to the ridiculous. The vast array of sports seen on this Sunday afternoon broadcast ranged from skating, to fishing, to drag racing, to one episode featuring a man who strapped dynamite to his chest, then blew himself up. (Thankfully, the man survived the stunt.)

Thanks to *CBS Sports Spectacular*, skaters were about to have access to far larger audiences and far greater fame than ever before. In the past, the top skaters were well known within a small community of serious fans and perhaps at least familiar to a wider audience of people who followed sports. Now the best performers, for the first time ever, would be household names throughout the country. The awareness of this new level of visibility and renown no doubt may have made some skaters more nervous than usual, while for others the event would have seemed like the opportunity of a lifetime.

Whatever you called it—"The U.S. Championships," or just plain "Nationals" as most skaters did—this event was by far the most important to date on the 1961 competition calendar, cameras or not. The competition wasn't just about winning medals or trophies, either. Winning a gold, silver, or bronze medal in the ladies, men's, pairs, or dance events meant a stronger chance of actually being seen in the televised portion of the championships. With only one hour to cover the four major disciplines, the broadcast editors could only concern themselves with the standout performances. Most important of all, however, was the opportunity a top-three finish presented. Finishing on the podium earned each of the victors a spot on the team that would represent the United States at two important competitions: the North American Figure Skating Championships and the World Figure Skating Championships.

The North American Championships no longer exist today, replaced by the more frequent "Grand Prix" events, but in 1961 the "North Americans" were considered a vital precursor to the World Championships. The North Americans that year would be held in Philadelphia. The team then would head for the World Figure Skating Championships to be held in Prague, Czechoslovakia. A trip behind the forbidding Iron Curtain would put the skaters in a very select group at a time when such travel was much more difficult and more expensive than it is today. Inclusion in that group, as every skater knew while warming up on that day in Colorado Springs, required earning a medal at the Nationals, where their years of training and sacrifice would come down to just a few minutes on the ice.

The pressure of making history rested on the shoulders of the vibrant Laurence Owen. It did not appear, however, to weigh her down. To the contrary, the poised bounce in her stride as she enjoyed her first day at the Broadmoor Ice Palace suggested a level of self-possession that certainly must have intimidated her competitors. Laurence was a girl who marched to her own rhythm. While always polite and mature in her manner of speech, she exuded an individualism and fierce independence that she, no doubt, inherited from her larger-than-life mother. Those qualities were manifest even in her appearance. She wore pants over her long legs much more often than the skirts favored by most girls of her time, and she kept her dark brown hair in a short, boyish pixie cut, a style uncommon for a teenager in the early sixties and one that seemed designed especially for her high cheekbones. Her eyes seemed to disappear into small slits when she flashed her large, toothy smile, called a "laughing smile" by photographers who had the pleasure to catch her in action. She looked exotic without being flashy and was wholesome and approachable. She spoke through her nose just a bit, like a lot of teenagers still discovering their voices, but she communicated her thoughts and feelings best with either a blank piece of paper or a vacant sheet of ice. Like her mother, she was half writer, half skater, and she'd often change her mind about which she liked better.

Laurence was part of a family figure-skating dynasty. Her mother, Maribel Vinson Owen, had won nine U.S. National Championships in the ladies event, six championships in the pairs event (along with three silver medal finishes), and had also won a silver medal in ice dance. She appeared in the Olympics three times and claimed a medal in one of those appearances, yet her legacy was

Photo courtesy of the Winchester Massachusetts Archival Center

Laurence, "Big Maribel," and "Little Maribel" Owen together.

unfulfilled, having never won the elusive gold medal. Laurence's late father, Guy Owen, had been a Canadian men's junior champion and North American champion in an event called "fours," which featured four skaters performing tricks in tandem—somewhat of a miniature precursor to what we now call "synchronized skating." Laurence's grandparents skated as well, and were members of the Figure Skating Club of Boston. Gertrude "Granny" Vinson even performed once for the Queen of England.

From its beginnings as a place for Boston's elite to socialize, "The Club," as it was known locally, rose to a level of dominance none of the nation's nearly thirty other clubs could match. Because skating drew most of its participants from the wealthier classes, the sport also meshed well with the Harvard community. Olympic gold medalists Dick Button and Tenley Albright, for example, were among the top U.S. skaters who earned Harvard degrees. In 2004, the Harvard Varsity Club's John Powers wrote about this bond.

"Rosy-cheeked Brahmins already had been doing figure eights for years on outdoor ice at the Cambridge Skating Club on Mount Auburn Street and The Country Club in Brookline. In a day when Harvard and Boston society were conjoined, it was inevitable that figure skating would wear a crimson muffler."

The Owen family played a leading role in the Boston skating scene's storied history. It was not surprising that the Vinson-Owen skating gene was emerging in a third generation—in Laurence, and her older sister, Maribel, Jr. They were not competing just for themselves; they were competing for their mother and for the one medal she had never won.

Even though the Olympic gold medal had eluded her, Maribel was viewed with the kind of reverence reserved for athletes with a legendary resume. As she led her daughters around the Broadmoor Ice Palace, whispers of fascination echoed through the corridors. "There she is!" "Laurence looks just like her mother!"

Maribel, known as "Big Maribel," on the skating scene, was a galvanizing figure. She was charming, intelligent, animated, and always willing to share her opinion. Former student Ron Ludington said those who were close to her cherished her as a beloved mother figure, but that others had trouble warming to her.

"She ran the show, and she was considered out of line. She wasn't supposed to behave that way. Others would say she behaved like a man."

Ludington added, "She opened a lot of doors. She took charge and it rubbed a lot of people the wrong way."

Ben Wright, skating historian and a mainstay of the Boston Club, agrees that Maribel had an outspoken side. "She did not waste words."

Maribel was known as a hard-driving coach. The built-in expectation to skate—and win—made the Owen family dynamic extremely harsh at times. She ran the house with a military sense of order that would drive the toughest army general to exhaustion. She was Auntie Mame and the Unsinkable Molly Brown wrapped up into one combustible soul. She was known as a woman who never minced words, even when it meant burning important bridges. She lived for the advancement of skating on all levels—but lived mostly for her daughters, for whom she worked tirelessly and whom she loved with her entire being. She wanted them to be successful—and in recognizing their tremendous talents, she sometimes could push both daughters to the brink. Laurence, effervescent and always happy on the outside, faced daunting pressure to fill her mother's legendary shoes.

Ron Ludington remembers Laurence as a tremendously friendly girl who had no trouble meeting new people.

"Laurence was outgoing and liked to talk to people, but she was a strong-willed person. Maribel and Laurence fought fiercely at times."

She always handled this pressure with a smile that masked all hardships, but the outwardly serene family home hid from the world the emotional tempests that exploded within. Despite the occasional mother-daughter tempests, Laurence and her mother were extremely close—and both found their greatest happiness on the ice.

Maribel, Jr., known as Mara to family and friends, was the calm voice of the house. She, too, was a champion, but she was growing wary of the sport. Mara had achieved success in the national pairs ranks beginning in 1956, when she won a bronze medal, but it was only when she teamed with debonair partner Dudley Richards that the delicate and wispy brunette showed her greatest potential. Together, they had won two bronze medals at Nationals, along with a silver medal in 1960. They had placed as high as sixth at the World Championships.

Mara's skating, however, had most certainly taken a backseat to her little sister's dramatic rise through the ranks. After all, only the singles skater could reach that mythic status of ice queen. Only the singles skater seemed to harness the public's imagination and adoration. Mara never fully developed as a singles skater, struggling to land all the perilous, high-impact jumps required of an ice queen. Her destiny was to become a pairs skater—one whose victories would be shared by a partner, and eclipsed by a more gifted younger sibling. The great love shared between these two sisters belied the great pain and disappointment Mara often felt while seeing the younger excel beyond her own capabilities. Chuck Foster, Mara's former pairs partner and a former president of the United States Figure Skating Association, said, "She often found herself outside of the publicity circle. It could be tough on her sometimes." Mara had one wonderful comfort, though. As her pairs partnership with Dudley matured, they became inseparable off the ice, too. It appeared Mara and Dudley were showing the preliminary sparks of a beautiful relationship in the making.

Mara, though shy and soft-spoken, still could raise her voice at times, showing the famous Owen family moxie when a particular passion arose in her. In fact, Mara made a very large impact on American skating that most skaters don't know about today. Up until 1959, World and Olympic teams were chosen based on the performance of the previous year. The U.S. National Championships were not held until after the World Championships, which many skaters of the day felt was tantamount to having the semifinals after the finals.

Mara disagreed with this policy. She felt it only made sense to hold Nationals, then allow the new champions to be presented on the world stage. This would also ensure that skaters in the best physical shape would represent the U.S. at Worlds. At the 1958 meeting of the U.S. Skating Governing Council in Boston, Mara spoke to the delegates and urged them to vote in favor of a new schedule that would put Nationals before Worlds. Remarkably, the council agreed with the fifteen-year-old. This decision gave a much-needed boost of confidence for a teenager who was at times so unsure of herself.

Chuck Foster marveled at her work at the Governing Council.

"Here's a kid getting up in front of the Governing Council, who single-handedly got the association to change the rules. It shows how a young person could sway people to change the system."

The Owen family was full of trailblazers, and in 1961, they were prepared to set a new standard in becoming the "first family" of American figure skating. If Mara and Laurence could win in their events, it would mark the first time a parent and child had won the same title in the history of the sport.

Mara and Dudley were the clear front-runners for the gold medal. As she walked around the Ice Palace, Mara seemed calm and relaxed. In fact, their pairs event generated little buzz at all compared to the ladies singles competition. When she walked the Broadmoor's hallways with her sister, it was Laurence who drew the looks and the whispers of recognition. Laurence's victory at the 1961 Nationals, however, was not assured by any stretch of the imagination. Her closest rival had just as many reasons to believe this was *her* year, too.

Chapter Two

As Stephanie Westerfeld walked through the Broadmoor Ice Palace, she felt right at home, down to the locker that belonged to her, to the concession stand workers who knew her name and greeted her like a favorite child. This was the rink where she had spent at least a third of every day for the last several years, and where she hoped to be crowned national champion.

"Steffi" was seventeen, seven months older than Laurence Owen, and just as talented. She represented the Broadmoor Figure Skating Club—the host club for the National Championships—and despite Laurence's considerable reputation, Steffi was a formidable challenger who many skating insiders felt was equally able to be American's next ice queen.

Where Laurence's enthusiasm and energy were raw and unfettered, Steffi was the snapshot of grace and softness in everything she did. She was somewhat shy, but still managed to be popular in school. She was a homecoming queen, a gifted pianist, and a straight-A student. She managed to excel at everything despite family upheaval that may have toppled a weaker person.

She was tiny—weighing only about a hundred pounds—and

had a round, cherubic face with glowing pink cheeks and a dimpled chin. Her honey-brown hair was perfectly curled just under her ears, her short bangs drawing attention to her brown, deep-set eyes. She had a high voice—like something that you'd hear from a windup doll—a voice that, from all accounts, was never used to utter an unkind word to anyone. She was the girl in high school who had it all—the looks, the grades, the grace, and the musical and athletic ability. She was quite accomplished, yet modest and never full of herself, instead possessing a kind of angelic quality.

The only demon she displayed was the one she'd unleash on herself. Steffi was, most of all, a perfectionist. Second place was considered failure in her eyes. Any grade lower than an "A" was not acceptable. Falling in a competition was cause for personal punishment. While skating gave her great joy, it could, in its frustrating moments, be her undoing. Perfection was the only key to Steffi's happiness. Until she could attain it, she would not relax.

Though friends called her an introvert, Steffi was becoming accustomed to star treatment. The local papers had written many stories about her successes on the ice. After a time, the papers stopped using her last name altogether, just calling her "Steffi." This attention may well have caused some students who attended Cheyenne Mountain High School to resent her. The school contained a wide-ranging mélange of economic and social classes—a real mix of the "haves" and "have-nots." Many of the students there skated at the Broadmoor Ice Palace—and because skating was so expensive, this gave the impression that the skaters were of the wealthier set. Many military families populated Colorado Springs, and some of the military children often felt like economic and social outcasts. Steffi never bought into the class system. Her focus on achieving her best in skating and all endeavors made it impossible to get caught up in the usual high school drama. She didn't have time for it.

Steffi's delicate persona concealed a desire that burned hot

Photo courtesy of Diane Yeomans Robins.

Stephanie Westerfeld had high championship hopes in 1961.

within her—a desire to pursue the Olympic dream. Steffi's dynamic mother, Myra, helped keep those dreams alive through her devotion to the sport and its role in her daughters' lives. Like Maribel, Myra's very existence revolved around her two daughters and their various skating pursuits. Steffi's older sister, Sharon, eight years Steffi's senior, had also pursued the Olympic dream, and fell short. Steffi had become a stronger skater than her sister, but in her previous attempts at achieving her dream, she had fallen short too, and Laurence was the cause.

Before the 1961 Nationals, Steffi and Laurence had met in

competition only one other time, and that was in 1960. Since Steffi lived in Colorado Springs and Laurence in Boston, they were never in the same competitive region—meaning they wouldn't have met in the sectional and regional competitions that qualified skaters to Nationals. Steffi and Laurence both advanced from their sectional meets to qualify for the 1960 U.S. Nationals. The top two American women seemed obvious—Carol Heiss and Barbara Roles. Carol was the reigning world champion, and Barbara had placed fifth in the world in 1959. With Heiss and Roles sure to win gold and silver, the bronze medal was the most coveted piece of hardware available to the lesser-known skaters.

Winning bronze put the world on notice about America's future in the sport. It would also earn the winner a trip to the 1960 Squaw Valley Olympics. Laurence and Steffi emerged as bronze medal front-runners. One of them would inevitably go home in a placement worse than dead last—fourth. In today's glamorous world of figure skating, even a fourth-place finisher in a deep field of talent can be asked to tour and even can become quite wealthy as a skater. These rare moneymaking opportunities were forbidden to skaters in 1960. Fourth place most assuredly equaled anonymity.

Laurence's mother drew attention to the strictness of the amateur rules in one of her three instructional skating books. In *The Fun of Figure Skating*, published in 1960, she is careful to mention in the opening pages that the skaters used to demonstrate technique in photos and illustrations "received no remuneration either directly or indirectly." In 1960, amateur guidelines had to be strictly followed, or athletes would face expulsion from the sport. There were no big-salary touring contracts, no television specials, or endorsement deals of any kind. The sport could not bring a penny of profit to the athlete, or else amateur status was revoked. One of the American ice dance competitors, Larry Pierce, had been forced to give up his job at the Coliseum ice skating rink in Indianapolis, because even his job resurfacing the ice constituted a violation of the rules.

Figure skaters were also expected to attend school full time. They did not have the tutors or home-schooling opportunities many sports stars have today. If they hoped to attend a good university, they had to be standout students. There were no figure skating programs at universities, so there were no scholarships connected to the sport.

In addition to the lack of compensation or rewards, there was a much slimmer chance of actually succeeding in a sport such as figure skating. Skating at the Olympics was and is all about the individual or pair. There is really no concept of "team," the way there is in soccer or basketball, in which a dozen players make up an Olympic or World delegation. Even Maribel Vinson Owen acknowledged the sacrifice and its frequent failure to bear fruit. "You could spend a decade on skating and only end up with heartbreak," she once told a student.

So why endure the sacrifices, the hardships, the long training hours, and the time away from family and friends? It's the athlete's creed to believe that one day the efforts will pay off. There is no room for self-doubt. There is no room to believe that fourth place is the best result possible. At the 1960 U.S. National Championships, only three young ladies could stand on the podium. Only three could go to the Olympics. If Heiss and Roles performed as expected, even if Laurence or Steffi did well, one would have to go home.

In the ladies and men's competitions, the judges awarded points in two segments: the compulsory figures—the esoteric pattern work carved into the ice—and the long program, also known as the free skate. In the latter segment, skaters chose their own music, as they do today, and performed the most visually appealing part of skating—the jumping, spinning, and choreography—in programs that last more than four exhausting minutes.

Compulsory figures, from which the name "figure skating" derives, were worth two-thirds of the overall score. Each move was based on the famous "figure eight" maneuver, in which an actual number "8" could be seen traced into the ice. Also called "school figures," there were many variations on this shape, some of which resembled snowflakes and stars. Each variation required a mastery of "edging." Each skate blade contains two edges—the inside and outside edge. Edges produce speed, power, and traction. A trained figure skater can look at the ice after a move and determine which edge touched the ice. Beginners often ride on the "flats" of the blades—that part of the steel between edges that keeps the speed slow and carves thick lines into the ice.

Figures demand control. They take a precise, steady blade, perfect placement of body weight, strong ankles and torso muscles, and correct timing to trace just the right marks into the ice. The figures consist of two or three circular lobes with different variations in position and edge of the blade. Some of the more complex figures required tracing a pattern, then retracing over it with the other foot. Judges looked for perfect, wobble-free circles, all with the same shape and diameter. The judges hovered nearby as skaters completed this portion of the competition, then they inspected the marks up close.

By the time the 1960 Nationals had arrived, Steffi was known as one of the best practitioners of figures in the country. Being as modest as she was, she nearly competed at the junior level in 1960 but decided instead that she should challenge herself and skate on the senior level. If she could perform her figures perfectly, a medal would be within reach. In fact, if her figures went well, she could create a sizeable enough lead over other bronze medal contenders to secure her Olympic berth before the free skate even began.

This lopsided kind of judging frustrated many fans, and ultimately led to the abandonment of school figures. American skater Janet Lynn, a superb artist on the ice who seemed to practically float along the surface, never won a World Championship or Olympic gold medal—largely because she was not strong in school figures.

At the 1972 World Championships, Austrian Beatrix Schuba had built such an enormous lead after the school figures that she won the gold despite placing ninth in the free skate. Lynn finished third after a breathtaking free skate performance.

Television helped lead to the demise of school figures. Because only the more visually exciting free skate was shown on television, audiences at home were confused and appalled by the outcome of the 1972 Worlds. The complaints were so abundant that the International Skating Union created what we now know as the short program to lessen the overall importance of figures in the final placements. The death knell for figures rang in 1990, when they were removed from international competition altogether. In their place, skaters are now required to perform what are known as "moves in the field," a mixture of dance steps, turns, edgework, and stroking. These moves are designed to show a command of both blade and body. They are not part of national or international competitions, but skaters do have to take proficiency tests in these moves in order to "graduate" to different levels of competition.

Laurence was similar to Janet Lynn in that she was known to be better in the free skate than in school figures. At the 1960 Nationals, Laurence performed admirably in the school figures, allowing Steffi to take only a slight lead for the bronze. The free skate would settle the matter As predicted, Carol Heiss and Barbara Roles won the gold and silver, respectively, and when the bronze medal was decided, Laurence bested Stephanie by only one sixteenth of a point.

Laurence was jubilant. Steffi was crushed. It would have been much easier to take had she finished near the bottom of the field. Finishing fourth, however, was truly painful; being first alternate was proof that Steffi did belong in the senior level, but they may as well have named it the "oh-so-close-but-you're-not-going-to-the-Olympics" award.

Courtesy of the U.S. Olympic Committee

The 1960 Squaw Valley Olympic Team included two members of the Owen family. Mara is second from left, and Laurence is third from left.

The Owen family celebrated not one, but two Olympics berths. In a fortuitous, but not entirely surprising, turn of events, Mara and Dudley had claimed the silver medal in the pairs event. Laurence's mother, as their coach, viewed this moment as an affirmation of her own coaching abilities. Her pride in her daughters' accomplishments was beyond measure.

It didn't seem possible to make Steffi a harder worker, but her fourth-place finish had just that effect. Her disappointment simmered for a year. She had something to prove at Nationals. She entered the Ice Palace in January of 1961 and began her customary routine of stretching in the hallways and performing off-ice jumps, sometimes getting so lost in her practice maneuvers that she didn't notice the people coming perilously close to her as she heaved herself into the air.

Steffi was the golden girl of the Broadmoor. Despite this, she must have felt like an underdog. The Boston club members stormed into the rink as if they owned it—swaggering around in big exclusive groups. They were fully aware that Boston's skating scene was synonymous with winning championships. All in all, the Colorado competitors viewed them as obnoxious and arrogant. Her competitive fire would not allow her to show her feelings, but Steffi was intimidated, especially after seeing what Laurence could do during practice.

Laurence had a slight advantage, anyway. She had, after all, already appeared in one Olympic Games and one World Championships. Laurence finished sixth at the 1960 Squaw Valley Olympics, and ninth at the World Championships (at Worlds, she was skating on an injured knee). Sports reporters at the time felt Laurence's dance elements were so modern the judges did not know how to score her in the Olympics. Laurence was not a skater to simply jump and spin to music. The music took hold of her soul and she interpreted it with an unabashed joy. The judges were not accustomed to this type of exuberance. Laurence's sister and pairs partner finished tenth in both the 1960 Games and Worlds.

In the 1960 Olympics, Laurence had her fair share of admirers. Carol Heiss, en route to her gold medal, shared a room with Laurence in the Olympic Village. Heiss recognized the younger skater's potential and knew she was on the cusp of a magnificent career.

Heiss told Laurence affectionately, "My time is over. I'll be looking forward to seeing you on the podium in the future."

Before she could skate her way to the podium in 1961, Laurence would endure a week of practice, final coaching sessions with her mother, and plenty of glares from other competitors who, underneath the polite smiles, seethed with jealously as they carried out the pre-competition ritual of sizing each other up.

Laurence and Steffi certainly knew of each other, and must have considered themselves the top two skaters, based on their finishes at the championships of the previous year. In an odd twist, both Laurence and Steffi almost didn't make it to the 1961 Nationals. A few months before the event, Laurence slipped, fell forward, and badly banged up her knee during practice. This was the same knee she'd hurt during the 1960 World Championships. For several weeks, the knee was swollen and bruised. She was beginning to have doubts that it would heal for Nationals, and to fear that she'd miss the chance to secure the family legacy that was so important. Finally, the swelling subsided and Laurence regained her jumps—and her confidence—just in time.

Steffi almost didn't make it to Nationals for other reasons. Her virtuoso skills at the piano had earned her first place at the Colorado State Piano Competition. She was asked to represent Colorado in the National Piano Competition. The timing could not have been worse. The piano event was happening the same week as Nationals. Steffi's goal was to be a concert pianist, and most agree she loved playing piano just as much, if not more, than skating, but she chose to skate at Nationals instead. She was eager to win a medal after barely missing the podium the year before.

Five judges were to score each event, using a 6.0 scale in each set of marks. They would award one mark for technical merit, and another for manner of presentation, what was later known as "artistic impression." The competition referee gave last-minute instructions to the judges, and the accountant made sure his adding devices were all calibrated and performing their critical task to perfection. These preparations were all carried out with no significant bobbles or missteps. Only one minor mishap occurred when the Russian-style fur hats given to judges for warmth caused an allergic reaction for one judge, who suffered sneezing fits and watery eyes.

In a last-minute panic, parents began to fear the ice rink wasn't perfectly level after some skaters complained of feeling off balance.

Even just a slight slope could throw off the body's natural timing. In the 2000 Sydney Summer Olympics, the gymnastics vault was set too low and many competitors had some scary misses on this apparatus. The outrage was understandable—in all sports, equipment must be set perfectly to ensure both safety and fair play. In ice skating, the most important piece of equipment besides the skates is the skating surface.

The rink manager approached the ice, nervously anticipating a drastic ice resurfacing, and placed a carpenter's level on the rink. A hushed crowd awaited the verdict. "The ice is perfectly level," the manager said, almost astonished.

With that piece of business now settled, the competition was ready to commence. Newspaper reporters interviewed competitors somewhat freely, in an era free of the talent agents, managers, and security now present in the world of elite figure skating.

Laurence, always modest, gushed about her outstanding mother to reporters.

"Mother deserves all the credit for our victories," she said. "We started on double runners at the age of two and formal lessons began at six. This means practicing as long as six hours a day. That sounds a like a lot of work, but we find it fun."

Laurence spoke with a sense of wonderment about skating, always beaming about the joy it brought her. Steffi, on the other hand, seemed less concerned with having fun and more on achieving her ultimate goals.

One Colorado Springs reporter asked Steffi for her final thoughts before skating.

"I have my heart set on a trip to Europe," she said. "If nothing unforeseen happens, I'll skate toward the 1964 Olympics."

Chapter Three

The most gifted artist could not paint a more striking landscape. A snow-capped mountain pierced the hovering clouds. Jagged rocks gave way to lush greenery as the mountain spread closer to earth. Pikes Peak, the jewel of the Colorado Rockies, stood high above Colorado Springs, a sleepy western town that had become a desirable destination for the emerging upper middle class and the decidedly well-to-do. It was here that the 1961 U.S. National Figure Skating Championships would take place. For many years, skiing was the only winter sport of note in the town—but that changed when the drama and beauty of figure skating captured the hearts of two of the town's most prominent citizens.

Near Pikes Peak, Cheyenne Mountain drew a select crowd of ski enthusiasts in the early 1900s. A small hotel and casino offered respite for the weary tourists, but Spencer and Julie Penrose, a fashionable and wealthy young couple, envisioned something better for the location. They purchased the hotel and transformed it into the most luxurious resort in the world, complete with a golf course, riding stables, and every other appointment of wealth.

The Broadmoor Hotel opened in 1918. Its pink stucco

Courtesy Pikes Peak Library District

The Broadmoor Ice Palace.

exterior beckoned guests to enter its luxurious halls. Its most distinctive feature was an opulent tower reaching into the sky. At the Broadmoor, presidents played and Hollywood stars roamed the halls after cotillions and socials. The hotel brought a touch of sophistication to the still untamed spirit of the West. The hotel flourished as the decades clicked by, and the area, in part because of the Broadmoor's classic European flair, earned the name "Little Switzerland."

In the late 1930s, one of the latest diversions of society was attending popular ice revues that included headliners like Frick and Frack, and the inimitable Sonja Henie, now at the peak of her brilliant career. Sonja cast a spell on Spencer and Julie Penrose when they saw her perform in 1937. They instantly fell in love with the ice and decided to bring skating to their posh hotel.

The Penroses tore out the Broadmoor's riding stables to make room for a new ice rink, a move that perplexed some of the guests but quickly drew even more attention to the hotel. With few all-year indoor rinks in the country, the new arena had a real chance to be the most state-of-the-art facility in the nation. With its arched exterior, imposing beams, and Olympic-sized ice surface, the Broadmoor Ice Palace lived up to expectations when it opened its doors to skaters in 1938.

Spencer and Julie Penrose wanted more than just a place for the rich to play. They wanted the arena to serve as a training ground for top competitors throughout the world. They also wanted the arena to play host to some of the biggest ice and hockey competitions. This message was duly conveyed to Broadmoor president Thayer Tutt (whose wife was an American skating champion). He worked as a tireless advocate for the Broadmoor, securing some of the biggest ice tournaments of the day. The World Figure Skating Championships came there in 1957 and 1959. In 1961, the Broadmoor Ice Palace was selected to host the U.S. National Figure Skating Championships.

As the finishing touches were being put on the facility in 1938, an Austrian émigré was working toward what he hoped would be a promising coaching career. Edi Scholdan, a diminutive man barely 5'6", spoke with a sharp Austrian accent that made him sound cold and austere. But by all accounts he was infinitely kind with comedy running through his veins.

He began skating at age twelve in his native Vienna. He once placed fifth in a world professional competition, but performing, rather than competing, was his real love. Financially hampered by strict amateur rules, the expenses became too much for him to continue his competitive career. He joined a traveling ice show in Europe, and his antics on the ice, from juggling to purposefully tripping over his own feet, brought him huge acclaim. Scholdan fed off of the immense laughter and joy.

Photo courtesy of Dixie Wilson

Edi Scholdan was one of the nation's best coaches, having molded two Olympic champions. He was Steffi Westerfeld's coach in 1961.

He decided to venture to the United States and try his hand at performing and coaching. Along the way, he served in the military police. His friend, Ice Follies performer Howard Deardorff, never could understand why they put such a funny person in the military police. Deardorff described Scholdan as a "helluva sweet guy. A loving bear."

In 1943 Scholdan and a fellow military officer found themselves in hot pursuit of an AWOL soldier. They were hopping trains, moving from town to town following leads for four months, when they spotted the man on a train. They took care not to let him know he had been discovered. While Scholdan's partner left the train to call the next town and arrange for a squad car, Scholdan sat down and started a conversation with the man, giving him no indication he was about to be arrested. For thirty minutes, they talked about their families, their hometowns, and their future plans. When they arrived at the next stop, Scholdan just said, "I guess you know that we recognize you." The AWOL soldier did not seem surprised. In fact, he thanked Scholdan for treating him with so much respect, and eagerly stretched out his hands for the handcuffs. The other officer was dumbfounded that their lengthy pursuit had ended so peacefully, with the help of Scholdan's charm.

After Scholdan had fulfilled his duty with the military, he found himself in the center of American luxury—the Broadmoor Hotel. He began coaching part time at the Broadmoor Ice Palace, then in 1948 was given a full-time contract. His coaching style was strict, but kind. He would jokingly chase his students around the ice with blade covers, then during lunch breaks would sit with them outside the rink and read the "Dear Abby" column with his own hilarious ad-libs. From these moments, he earned the nickname "the clown prince of Broadmoor."

He made his students laugh, but when it came to training, everyone knew who was boss. And his methods began to produce stunning results. By 1956, less than a decade after taking a job at the Ice Palace, he had produced his first Olympic gold medalist in Hayes Alan Jenkins. Four years later, Hayes's little brother David won a gold medal, too. Scholdan's formula for success seemed to be working. Skaters from around the country were eager to study with him and his other talented colleagues. Edi and the beautiful rink where he was head coach made a fateful impression on a well-to-do family from Kansas City.

Lured by the beauty of Colorado Springs, Otto and Myra Westerfeld took their two daughters to the mountain retreat for a summer respite. During the Westerfeld family vacation to the Broadmoor, Steffi's older sister Sharon, called Sherri, was first exposed to skating, and the love was instant. The family returned to Kansas City, where Sherri was eager to visit a local ice rink, the Pla-Mor.

In the early fifties, the Pla-Mor was one of only a handful of indoor ice rinks in the country. In the winter, it was filled with skaters in the height of their competitive seasons, and in the summer months, it was converted into an indoor swimming pool.

Jane Bucher Jones was one of the competitive skaters in training at the Pla-Mor rink. Bucher Jones practiced her school figures with meticulous attention to detail, working hours on end to perfect the art. One day while practicing, she noticed a little girl copying her moves—with astonishing precision.

"If you've ever seen children skate, those who have good ankles are natural, in the sense that they don't have to overcome the weakness. I don't know whether she had 'dance' or not, but she just had that natural ability."

That little girl was Sherri Westerfeld. Sherri had the ankles—and the daring—that allowed her to try skating tricks, even though she had never had lessons before in her life.

Bucher Jones recalled, "I would do a spin and Sherri would do a spin, or three turns and stuff like that."

Bucher Jones decided in her own mind that Sherri had star quality and something needed to be done about it.

"I approached Sherri's mother, Myra," Bucher Jones recalled, "and I told her Sherri had so much natural talent."

Myra immediately enrolled Sherri in skating lessons, and took

Photo courtesy of Diane Yeomans Robins

Sharon Westerfeld pins a test medal on Steffi.

an active role in Sherri's development as a skater, even though she had never been a competitive skater herself. It was simply Myra's protective nature to stay at her daughters' sides at all times.

She doted on the girls. She had lost a son in infancy, and gave birth to Sherri at age thirty-one, and Steffi at age thirty-nine.

As Sherri blossomed into a talented world-class competitor

Steffi watched as her big sister would soar through the air, spin, and earn praise and attention. Steffi would receive attention as the cute little girl at the rink, so fond of the concession-stand popcorn that she came to be known as "Popcorn." With her curly locks, she at some moments resembled another gifted child—Shirley Temple.

Steffi wanted to do more than just wait on the sidelines. At four years old, she asked her mom if she could skate, too. Myra agreed, and Steffi laced up and began taking lessons. In her very first competition, she finished dead last out of eighteen skaters, and declared she "hated" skating. She eventually recaptured her ambition and never finished in last place again.

Both Westerfeld girls were showing immense talent. They were easily the most talented competitive skaters in Kansas City, but the geography of their birth hindered their development in the sport. It was impossible to attract any famed coaches to Kansas City because the rink, only open in the fall and winter, could not pay a coach's salary all year. Former U.S. Nationals competitor Bill Swallender coached there for only a few seasons because he needed full-time pay.

No one anticipated the elite qualities that would emerge in Sherri's and Steffi's skating. To maintain and improve upon these gifts, the girls would need to train in the summer months, too. The Westerfelds' eyes turned back to the Broadmoor, a fertile ground for champions. The opportunity to train with a world-class coaching staff on a prestigious ice surface would factor heavily into whatever decision the family would make.

The finances were such that family patriarch Otto Westerfeld could afford to send Myra and the girls to Colorado Springs in the summer months. In 1949, they rented an apartment and stayed there during the summer. This pattern repeated itself the next summer, with Otto visiting frequently.

Sherri's skating blossomed, and her little sister was showing potential, too. Even though Steffi was only five years old, she was willing to try anything. You could sense a hunger in her childlike repetitions of her big sister's moves. Steffi was soon enrolled in skating lessons, too.

With two children desperate to stay in skates all year, Myra and Otto were left with few options. Edi had a magical way of explaining things that made everything come together for Sherri, and it was not beneficial to have two different coaches in two different cities. Consistency in instruction is a key to success in any sport.

The Westerfeld family business was in Kansas City. Simply relocating and finding a new job was not an option. The decision was made to split the family—Otto would be the lone Westerfeld to remain in Kansas City, and the women would live in Colorado Springs full time, a unique arrangement for an American family in the early 1950s.

The Westerfeld women settled in quickly, and Sherri's progress proved the permanent move was worth it. In 1955, an eighteen-year-old Sherri was a top contender for a medal at the U.S. National Championships. She was even "going steady" with Olympic bronze medalist Jimmy Grogan, the perennial runner-up to Dick Button at the U.S. Nationals. Life was full of possibilities for the blossoming young woman.

Throughout these years, Otto continued to visit. He sent weekly checks to cover the costs for skating, housing, and other expenses, never leaving Myra and the girls waiting for anything. The Westerfelds seemed like the picture of the American dream—happy, affluent, and with two youngsters well on the road to athletic fame. The only obvious ingredient missing from this formula was that Otto did not live under the same roof as his family. Myra was the leader of the household, and Otto was in many ways a part-time husband and a reliable funding source. Myra, as sole parent living in Colorado, spent all her days keeping vigil at the Ice Palace, watching

Photo courtesy of Diane Yeomans Robins

Stephanie and mother Myra Westerfeld.

every lesson, critiquing every move, and drilling important training reminders into the girls' heads well into the night. Over time, Myra became completely wrapped up in the girls' skating—everything from the jumping and figures technique, to the costumes she had custom-made for their competitions. While pushing her daughters to be more disciplined, she nonetheless was charming and funny, and most of the time, people loved to be around her. She endeared herself to people by calling them "sugar" and remembering every little detail about their lives, giving a sense that she really was a kind of rink mother to everyone.

Myra's dreams were about to be realized in 1955, when Sherri reached the apex of her ability leading up to the U.S. Nationals. Sherri was a strong competitor in school figures, but often struggled in the free skating portion of the event. After a successful compulsory figures round that put a medal well within reach, she did not execute her free skate well, missing some key jumps and opening the door to other competitors.

She ended up placing in the dreaded position of fourth. Tenley Albright was the winner, Carol Heiss was second, and Catherine Machado took the bronze—the first time a Hispanic American had won a medal in American figure skating. All the years of sacrifice had left Sherri exhausted and wearing the unfortunate title of first alternate.

The top finishers did end up competing at Worlds, so Sherri's alternate position provided no real reward. She quit competitive skating to attend Colorado College, where she planned to earn a degree in psychology. She was no longer interested in the rigors of competitive skating, and was content to watch her little sister gradually prove herself as a far more gifted skater. Sherri loved skating—but did not particularly enjoy competing. She thought that maybe someday she could get a job with one of the big touring companies. She stayed close to the rink through college, even coaching part time.

Steffi's skating, meanwhile, was improving beyond anyone's wildest expectations. She passed her gold freestyle test—the "final exam" that allows a skater to compete at the senior level nationally. She was one of the hardest workers anyone at the Broadmoor had ever seen. At 4:30 a.m., she rose from sleep, went to the rink, and practiced for three hours until it was time for school. She immediately returned to the rink after school and spent another two to three hours practicing. From there, she went home, ate dinner, practiced piano, and did her homework. If she was lucky, she might have enough energy left to attend a school dance or see a movie. But that kind of luck was rare. With the 1961 U.S. Nationals looming in the distance, Steffi could not afford to relax and give up any training time. With her mother always at her side, it would have been difficult to slow the pace.

For several years now, Steffi had been living without a father figure in the house. More and more, she looked at coach Edi Scholdan as the predominant male influence in her life. He believed in her. She respected him. She relied on this relationship even more when life took a sour turn.

About a year before the 1961 Nationals, Otto stopped sending those vital checks. Myra inquired, but Otto could never give a straight answer. If Myra suspected he was having an affair, she certainly did not humiliate herself by mentioning it publicly. With no money coming in at the most critical time in Steffi's burgeoning career, the Broadmoor Figure Skating Club pitched in to pay for Steffi's ice time and lessons. Edi would sometimes instruct her for free. To pay for Steffi's training and other family expenses, Sherri, now a college graduate, took a job at a local jewelry store. Sherri had aspired to be a choreographer with the Ice Capades, but she put her own dreams on hold to help her sister.

Myra, accustomed to being affluent and comfortable, suddenly found herself taking handouts—from her own daughter and from anyone else who sympathized with their sudden plight. This humbled her, and made her even more dependent on her daughters for both emotional and financial stability. Somehow, Steffi had to block out the lingering questions about her parents and the embarrassment over finances to train for her big moment, just months away. Even small distractions can translate into dangerous mistakes on the ice, so her unraveling family fortune had terrible potential to interfere with her training.

Finally, Otto Westerfeld announced he was divorcing Myra and marrying another woman—a much younger woman, barely older than twenty-four-year-old Sherri. Though the Westerfelds had physically lived apart for several years now, the stigma of divorce was hard to swallow for them. In that era, divorce rates were low, largely because of gender roles that required women to simply accept whatever their husbands decided. Myra's largest sphere of influence centered on her daughters and their skating. With her marriage ending, her last chance to succeed at anything depended on Steffi. The pressure must have been suffocating, but Steffi remained composed and mature throughout the ordeal, although she did occasionally show the depth of her feelings, usually by confiding in her older sister.

It is not clear when Otto began romancing the younger woman. Regardless, it seemed that there had always been three members of the Westerfeld marriage. Skating was the mistress, its seductive lure of future glory pulling the Westerfeld family apart at its once-solid foundation.

Otto's role in Sherri and Steffi's lives declined sharply after the divorce proceedings began. Sherri felt especially betrayed, and a rift developed. It was during these trying times that Sherri's life took an interesting turn. She married her boss at the jewelry store, an Italian immigrant named Roberto Agnolini. As far as family and friends knew, there had been no courtship, no developing romance. Differing accounts exist as to the nature of this marriage, which seems to have been done to secure Agnolini's ability to stay and work in the United States. Sherri never moved in with her husband, and there is some question about whether Myra or Steffi even knew about the marriage. Sherri may have kept it a secret, particularly from Myra.

Steffi, meanwhile, through her loyalty to her father and desperate need of his approval, found herself caught between two battling parents. Making the situation even worse, Myra began to blurt out hateful things about Otto at the rink. This new and very public disdain for Otto, combined with Myra's constant vigil over and commentary about her skating, annoyed Steffi, who by nature was both a private person and one who set very high standards for herself. Arguments between the teenager and her mother grew more frequent. Sherri, always ready with a cheerful phrase to encourage her sister, was the mediator in these arguments. Sherri was the calming influence in Steffi's life, and the two sisters, though eight years apart in age, grew closer through the turmoil.

Steffi found solace on the ice, where younger pupils often followed her around asking, "How do you do such lovely tricks?" Edi had to remind the youngsters that Steffi needed time for her own practice.

One bright spot during these painful times was the presence of a new family pet. The Westerfeld women named the black French poodle "Seric," which was short for "Sir Eric of Broadmoor." Myra and Sherri kept the dog with them at the rink sometimes and he became the Broadmoor's unofficial mascot.

The Westerfelds had one last shot to make it to the World Championships and the Olympics. Steffi's success would validate the enormous sacrifices that had been made and show that they had been, in the end, worth making. Yes, the 1961 Nationals were three full years away from the next Olympics, but following any Olympic year, there is always great anticipation about who will fill the shoes of former champions. The top performers, including Steffi and Laurence, were eager to stand out in a mostly unknown competitive field and to fill the places left open by those who had moved on from the sport.

Steffi and Laurence both did the same jumps and spins, but they had vastly different styles. Steffi's skating was perhaps more pure than Laurence's emotionally nuanced routines. Steffi had a gentle style that had a universal appeal. On the ice, she was like a Monet painting—soft lines, gentle shades, an airiness. Laurence, on the other hand, was like a Picasso—bold, unpredictable patterns, strong colors, very abstract. The skating purists of the world likely would have found Steffi more pleasing to watch, but Laurence skated with such remarkable panache she captivated an audience.

The stage was set for a dramatic showdown between dozens of competitors, but the stakes seemed highest for two families, the Owens and Westerfelds, whose members, in many ways, were mirror images of each other. Devoted, driven, and dynamic single mothers far ahead of their time, set out on a daunting, lifelong quest to achieve the best result for their overachieving daughters in the face of family tragedy. The elder daughters, often the mediators in their frenetic worlds, set the pace in skating, but never reached the skill level of the younger siblings, on whose shoulders the most thrilling golden hopes rested. On January 25, 1961, the lives of these women would be forever changed as they pursued what only one could have—the gold medal, and the royal title of America's new ice queen.

Chapter Four

Athletes from around the globe descended on the small, snowy mountain enclave of Lake Placid, New York, population four thousand. The year was 1932, and the occasion was the very first Olympic Games to take place on United States soil.

Maribel Vinson, America's reigning ice queen, had been training for this moment since she was a little girl. She possessed a mastery of school figures, sure and steady jumps, elegant spins, and speed. Maribel also had a nemesis—Sonja Henie. "She already has one Olympic gold medal," Maribel must have thought impatiently. "Why is she going for a second?"

Lake Placid Olympic organizers were eager to impress the world in their role as host, despite that fact that the village was going broke getting ready for the Games—so broke, in fact, that the president of the Olympic organizing committee, Dr. Godfrey Dewey, donated land owned by his family to be used for construction of a bobsleigh run.

Just three years into the Great Depression, it hardly seemed logical to be spending bundles of money on an athletic competition. The soup kitchen lines and abandoned lumber mills in nearby towns were not far from the Olympic venues. Because cities had placed bids for the Games well before the economic catastrophe, there was no turning back. The Olympic Games, in their short modern history, had already amassed a great deal of respect and prestige among all nations who participated, and brought about a goodwill among nations for which there was no price tag.

Europeans, especially those from the Nordic countries, dominated winter sports in the early twentieth century, but that did not assure that all the most competitive athletes would come to Lake Placid. Traveling from Europe to the States was difficult and expensive. Commercial aviation wasn't yet commonplace, and tickets on an ocean liner were costly. For these reasons, an almost embarrassingly tiny delegation from across the Atlantic even bothered to show up. Two hundred fifty-two athletes from seventeen countries were present, most from the United States or Canada. Only twenty-one of the competitors were women, and fifteen of those women were figure skaters. This unbalanced ratio was a testament to the social status of women—whose more accepted place was at home raising children, rather than bouncing around on a sports field in front of audiences.

Aside from the abysmal attendance numbers, unseasonably warm weather for a February in the Adirondacks delayed many of the events. Some of the events didn't even wrap up until days after the closing ceremonies. Because of the melted mountainside mess, snow had to be shipped from Europe and Canada to assure the downhill skiing events could go on as planned. By the time the competitors reached the bottom of the hill, their skis splashed down in puddles of slush. This emergency snow import also added to the already bursting budget of these Games.

Though a disaster on many important levels, the Lake Placid Games were also triumphant and majestic for many a participant and fan. The governor of New York, Franklin Delano Roosevelt,

Courtesy of the U.S. Olympic Committee

The 1932 U.S. Olympic ladies skating team. Maribel Vinson is seen second from right.

kicked off the opening day celebration with a resounding welcome to competitors from all nations. First Lady Eleanor became part of the Olympic spectacle by rolling up her petticoat and charging down the bobsleigh course for a pre-competition test run. She emerged without injury, if a bit queasy.

American Eddie Eagan dazzled crowds while winning his second gold medal in the four-man bobsleigh event. His first gold medal came at the summer Olympics in 1920, in boxing. He remains the only person ever to win gold medals in both a summer and winter Olympics.

The competitors in the figure skating and hockey events enjoyed a treat that was somewhat rare on the international competitive circuit—they would skate at an indoor facility, a huge brick field house built especially for the Olympics. Its new ice surface sparkled like diamonds. It was so perfect and lovely that one could almost feel a kind of guilt about disturbing its stillness. Condensation rose from the surface and created a mist that made the skaters appear to be apparitions floating by in a delicate dance.

As is the case with modern Olympics, the figure skating competition attracted the lion's share of publicity and interest. The competition in 1932 carried a special fascination. This was the year Norwegian Sonja Henie would compete in her third Olympics—and vie for a second gold medal. Organizers charged admission just to watch the practice sessions, and they brought in standing-room-only crowds.

A frustrated Maribel would have to face Sonja again. She had never beaten Sonja before and knew it was unlikely this time. Maribel's medal prospects were good. Her gold medal prospects, however, were slim, and she knew it.

"Sonja's routine is not as hard as mine, but she seldom makes a mistake," she groused to her coach.

Maribel's frustration was understandable. While she dominated on U.S. soil in the ladies event, and was a consistent top-three finisher in both pairs and dance, she never became a big name internationally. It seemed that the longer she honed her craft, the more difficult it became to win on the international stage. Following the 1928 season in which she won a silver medal at the World Championships, her career didn't take off the way she had hoped. Injured in 1929, Maribel wasn't able to compete at the World Championships to contend for a medal. In 1930, she returned to Worlds and won a bronze. In the next few years, she barely missed the podium. No one could doubt her work ethic, but her nerves seemed to play a role in her downward slide in the rankings. Maribel simply didn't perform consistently under pressure. Sonja Henie, though, seemed to thrive on pressure. Sonja won the gold at

Getty Images

Maribel Vinson performs in the Olympics.

every European and World competition, while Maribel struggled to place in the top five. It seemed that there was no end in sight to Sonja's dominance.

Many skaters of the television age—Tara Lipinski, Kristi Yamaguchi, Oksana Baiul, and Scott Hamilton—are content to win an Olympic gold medal and move on to the next phase of life, whether it be professional skating, coaching, or the extremely lucrative motivational speaking circuit. Winning one gold medal is good enough for most athletes—the odds against them are incredibly long. Winning two gold medals in figure skating is like scaling Mount Everest—twice.

Sonja, however, wanted to be the center of attention at all times. To have one gold medal in her coffers wasn't enough. She wanted a score of punctuation marks added to her dominance. The outside world knew her as gentle, caring, and compassionate, but her fellow competitors knew her dimpled smile concealed a bossy, diva-like temperament, and a cutthroat approach to any competitive situation.

Sonja, the darling curly blonde with unquestionable cuteness, started showing promise as a figure skater at a very early age. Her wealthy parents, especially her over-attentive father, indulged her every whim, often at the expense of her siblings, who received much less attention from their father. She even had her own private pond on which to practice. She took ballet lessons from some of the most respected prima ballerinas available to teach.

Sonja won her first Norwegian national championship at age eleven. Because no age requirement had been established for Olympic competition, in 1924, Sonja was already heading to her first Olympics. While competing, she stopped her program repeatedly, skated to the edge of the lake, and asked her coach what she should do next. The audience was overwhelmed by her charm, but the judges ranked her dead last out of only thirteen total competitors. There the flame was fully ignited.

While other skaters in that 1924 Olympics were wearing skirts that touched their ankles, Sonja was dressed as a little girl was expected to dress—in a pleated white skirt that stopped just above the knees. She was the picture of innocence. In addition to deciding she would win her next Olympics, she had also decided never to wear a full-length skirt while skating. With her shorter, children's skirts, she discovered she had more freedom of movement. She also decided she liked the white skating boots much better than the black boots that were customary for skaters of both genders. Already, Sonja was a trailblazer and a trendsetter.

Figure skating was not always about the grace and athleticism that Sonja and Maribel espoused. In fact, skating was not conceived as a sport at all; it was designed to be a mode of transportation. The early fishermen and hunters of northern Europe strapped animal bones, antlers, and wood onto their feet to glide across frozen lakes, a practice dating back to 300 A.D. In 1572, skates found their way onto the battlefield. Spain occupied the Netherlands, but the Dutch began their revolt when Spanish rulers would not tolerate the Reformation's spread into Holland. In the Battle of Ijsselmeer, the Dutch surprised the more powerful Spaniards by skating the frozen canals for combat. When the Spaniards attempted to use skates in the next round of battle, they fell all over themselves. Spain eventually lost the war. One could say then that skating played a role, albeit small, in the spread of Protestantism in Europe.

As the centuries progressed and modes of transportation became more sophisticated, skating evolved into a recreational pastime. Iron replaced animal bones as the blade of choice in the mid-1500s. In 1850, steel blades came along, but they had to be strapped onto normal boots. The next design was a slight improvement, with the blades attached to a wooden plate, which was then strapped to boots. Neither design allowed for much maneuverability or balance.

A revolutionary American changed that. Jackson Haines created a prototype of what we now recognize as modern skates—with the blades actually screwed into the boots. The toe pick (the teeth of the blade) came courtesy of English ironworker Henry Boswell in 1883.

Haines's legacy goes far beyond equipment. He is credited with merging artistry and skating. Up to that point, figures were the only skill performed on the ice. Haines was trained in ballet and saw great potential to merge dance and skating.

Before the creation of the United States Figure Skating Association, Haines won the Championships of America is 1863 and 1864. He wore what at the time was considered a "fancy" costume, and even performed the first-ever "sit spin," a spin performed by hovering as near to the ice as possible with one leg extended in front of the body.

Haines's flamboyance was not well received in war-ravaged America. Considered an oddity of sorts, he sailed to Europe, where he delighted audiences. He was particularly popular in Austria, where the Strauss family of composers wrote waltzes for him. Thomas Edison's phonograph wasn't invented until 1877, so Haines hired musicians to play at the side of the rink. It is believed Haines is the first to have skated to music.

Legend suggests Haines died in Finland in 1875 after catching pneumonia on a sled trip from St. Petersburg, Russia, to Stockholm, Sweden. Scholars, however, insist he died a much less glamorous death—caused by tuberculosis.

The first World Figure Skating Championships were held more than twenty years after Haines's death, in 1896. The event was held in St. Petersburg, Russia. Only men competed that year, although there was no rule precluding women from coming.

In 1902, a woman named Florence Madeleine Cave Syers (popularly known as "Madge"), of Great Britain, entered the World Championships in Sweden. She won the silver medal, nearly upsetting the home country's champion, Ulrich Salchow (inventor of the Salchow jump). After this event, the International Skating Union officially banned women from competition.

A change of heart ensued, and in 1906, ladies were invited to compete in the International Skating Union (ISU) Championships. Ladies were expected to keep their ankles covered, as was customary in that era. Madge Syers easily won the title in 1906 and 1907. In 1908, pairs skating became the newest discipline. Ladies, men, and pairs competed in the 1908 Summer Olympic Games in London. (There was not yet a Winter Olympics, so skaters were invited to the Summer Games.) Madge Syers became the first ladies Olympic gold medalist in figure skating. She also won a bronze in pairs with her husband/coach Edgar Syers. Ulrich Salchow won the gold for the men. Anna Hubler and Heinrich Berger of Germany won the first-ever Olympic pairs title.

There was no figure skating in the 1912 summer Olympics, because the host city, Stockholm, did not have an indoor ice facility. In 1916, there were no Olympics at all because of World War I, but skating was featured in an early movie. German skater Charlotte Oelschlagel, who won the adoration of the American public despite fierce anti-German sentiments, starred in the first movie featuring skating. In this 1916 serial movie, *The Frozen Warning,* Charlotte helped police find some no-good foreign agents by tracing the word "spies" into the ice, and pointing at the offenders. Charlotte was a sensational success, and starred in the first long-running ice show on American soil.

In 1920, skating was included in the Antwerp, Belgium, Summer Olympics. During this event, American Theresa Weld-Blanchard became the first woman ever to perform a jump in competition. It was a single Salchow, a jump requiring the skater to turn on one foot, then push off that same foot for one midair rotation. It's a difficult jump to perform, but Theresa did it wearing a full-length skirt. She was reprimanded by the referee for doing something so "unladylike." Weld-Blanchard took home a bronze medal, anyway, despite the rebuke.

In 1924, ladies and pairs became part of the World Championships. That same year, figure skating was included in the official program of the first Olympic Winter Games, held in Chamonix, France. That is where Sonja Henie burst onto the scene as that darling little rich girl with the golden locks.

Like Sonja, Maribel was a child of privilege. As a toddler, she watched her mother and father, Gertrude and Thomas Vinson, glide across the serene ponds of Winchester, Massachusetts. Her parents had met for the first time while skating. Their courtship blossomed on the ice. They were both members of one of America's first figure skating clubs, the Skating Club of Boston, where membership was offered only to the elite members of society, as with any country club. Thomas was a successful state legislator, which afforded the Vinson family a certain upper-class status.

The Vinson family lived in a stately colonial brick house at 195 High Street. Almost big enough to be a mansion, it was still a cozy home for Maribel, an only child. Encouraged by her parents, Maribel took to the frozen ponds near her home at a very young age, and started to excel in her early teens. She won her first U.S. national singles title in 1928 at age sixteen, and went on to win eight more championships. She also won several national medals in pairs and dance events, proving her great versatility.

Throughout her skating career, Maribel had shown brilliance as a student, especially when it came to writing. She decided she wanted to someday become a professional writer. She earned early admission to Radcliffe College in Boston, an honor given to only the brightest students. Radcliffe was considered one of the most prestigious women's schools in the Northeast. Harvard did not admit women at the time, and so a group of Harvard educators formed a group that chartered its own college, where women would receive the same quality of education as offered at the men's school.

Maribel rose to the occasion and graduated *cum laude*—an amazing feat, considering she never stopped her training regimen, which demanded six hours of ice time each day, usually beginning between four and five in the morning.

In 1932, Maribel won another U.S. National title and prepared for her next big challenge—the Olympics. She had placed fourth out of twenty in the 1928 St. Moritz, Switzerland, Olympics when she was only sixteen. Many people were impressed that she was so composed at such a young age, but Sonja Henie, younger and prettier, eclipsed Maribel. It seemed there wasn't room for newspaper reporters to write about two teenage skating phenoms. In 1932, Maribel was determined to win a medal this time around.

Dressed in a knee-length black frock with white lace trim, Maribel took to the ice for her long program. One by one, she ticked off the elements with polish. In this era, those elements consisted solely of single jumps, unlike the amazing triple jumps we see today. (Men are now doing quadruple jumps.) Skate boots reached three to four inches above the ankle, and were not nearly as supportive as today's hard boots.

Maribel had managed the most difficult single jump of all—the Axel, named for speed skater Axel Paulson. This jump is treacherous because it takes off going forward, and it is technically a revolution-and-a-half. Because of the extra half-revolution, many skaters need a long period of adjustment for the special timing it takes to do the Axel. All other jumps take off going backward.

Once her routine was complete, Maribel politely curtsied to the judges and the audience members. This was the best she had ever performed since winning a silver medal at the 1928 World Championships in London, where the royal family was so taken with her that they asked her to perform for them privately. Sonja had won first at that competition, too. But could Sonja beat Maribel's seamless performance this time?

Sonja skated onto the ice in a rich green pleated dress that didn't quite touch her knees. The dress was tapered at her waist and tight through the chest, highlighting her beautiful curves. The emerald color of the dress was the perfect shade for her golden blonde locks.

When Sonja skated, she truly took flight. Her technique was strong, but it was her artistry that clearly set her apart from other skaters. Her wealth afforded her the greatest dance instructors—including Russian ballerina Anna Pavlova. Her classical lines, infused with outright flirtation with the audience, made for a magnificent, mesmerizing mélange of glamour and sport. The judges had been

Hulton Archive/General Photographic Agency/Getty Images

Maribel Vinson performs a move called a "spread eagle."

cast under her spell, too. When the scores had been tallied, Maribel finished behind Sonja Henie. In fact, Maribel earned the bronze medal, with Fritzi Burger of Austria winning the silver.

Many sportswriters of the day felt Maribel was the true champion that year as far as overall skating technique. The mostly European judges disagreed. Whispers of favoritism threatened to be the next big disaster of the Lake Placid Games. The controversy never really picked up steam, but Maribel's deep-rooted suspicion of judges, one she would carry for the rest of her life, began here.

With two gold medals, Sonja was expected to leave the amateur ranks and turn professional. For that reason, Maribel made the commitment to skate toward one more Olympics, with the goal of competing in both the ladies and the pairs events.

After her graduation from Radcliffe, her parents encouraged her to pursue a life outside of skating. Her studies and training both proved she had a tremendous work ethic. One obvious career choice would be to coach skating, but she wanted to write, and she landed a history-making first job.

In 1934, twenty-two-year-old Maribel became the first female sportswriter in the history of the *New York Times*. Maribel must have shuddered with excitement at the history she was creating. She always met her deadlines and impressed even her hard-nosed boss, while her skill surprised even the more seasoned news veterans. The deadline for the 1936 Olympics was looming. She always found a way to sneak to the nearest ice rink at four in the morning. This would be a cruel and unusual form of punishment to most people with a full-time job, but to Maribel, this time on the ice was her only peace and quiet during the whole day. It was her sanctuary. She was preparing for her final appearance in the Olympics, and this time, she had also earned the right to compete in the pairs event with her partner, George Hill.

Contrary to prediction, Sonja Henie kept competing at the world level after the 1932 Olympics. She had won every single World Championships she had entered since 1927. No skater had ever won three Olympic skating titles. Sweden's Gillis Grafstrom just missed out when Austrian teen Karl Schafer barely edged him for a third gold at the 1932 Olympics.

The German villages of Garmisch and Partenkirchen were hosting the 1936 Winter Olympics. The International Olympic

Committee nearly revoked the Games from Germany because of the new Nazi regime's exclusionary policies toward Jewish athletes. When Hitler's government agreed to allow German Jews to compete, the IOC agreed to let the games go on as scheduled.

The figure skating venue was outdoors. Sonja Henie was already so popular that the police had to escort her to and from the venue. After the school figures, a fifteen-year-old British girl was only three points behind Sonja, and a threat for the gold. Sonja was not accustomed to having anyone so close to her in the standings. In the free skate, she performed with her usual charisma and flair, in an elegant white fur-trimmed costume that became the fashion statement of the Games. The crowd fell in love with her, and she won her third Olympic gold medal, a feat that has not been matched since. Despite her record-breaking win, she faced heavy criticism by the Western press when she bowed to Adolf Hitler and gave the Nazi salute after her performance. The medalists were instructed to bow to Hitler again as he placed the medals around their necks. Only the bronze medalist, Sweden's Vivi-Anne Hulten, refused to salute him. Hitler locked eyes with her for a full minute before he finally relinquished the medal to her.

Maribel was not put in this precarious situation, since she placed a disappointing fifth. She also placed fifth in the pairs event. Her best Olympic finish was the bronze medal she had won in 1932. Even if she had found the stamina to compete in a fourth Olympics, she didn't have the chance. World War II resulted in a long pause for the Olympics. In fact, it would be another twelve years before they returned, in tranquil St. Moritz, Switzerland. In three consecutive Olympics, Sonja Henie blocked Maribel's dreams. Maribel never uttered an unkind word about her publicly, but privately she confided that she disliked Sonja's arrogant, attention-loving personality.

"Sonja mania" had officially come ashore in America. Following the 1936 Olympics, Maribel had the task of reviewing her chief rival in the *New York Times*. The review was of Sonja Henie's first professional performance in New York. Sonja chose "The Swan" by Camille Saint-Saens.

"The crowd settled quickly into a receptive mood for Sonja's famous interpretation of the Dying Swan of Saint-Saens," Maribel wrote. With spotlights giving the ice the effect of water at night, Miss Henie, outlined in a blue light, performed the dance made immortal by Pavlova.

"Whether one agrees that such posturing is suited to the medium of ice, there is no doubt that Miss Henie's rendition is a lovely thing. Too much toe work at the start leaves the feeling that this does not belong to skating, but when she glides effortlessly back and forth, she is free as a disembodied spirit and there is an ease of movement that ballet never can produce."

A mostly objective account, her cynicism of Sonja's style did shine through a bit. Not long after the review was published, Maribel left the *Times* for a career in professional figure skating. There were very few opportunities to skate professionally at the time, and what opportunities did exist demonstrated a great divide between the "professional" skaters and the amateurs who had competed at the Olympics. Many touring professionals had never skated in the competitive ranks. They entertained crowds with moves such as barrel-jumping, hardly the kind of dignified, purist skating seen in international competitions.

Maribel founded two ice revues—first the International Ice Revue, then Gay Blades. She toured North America with men's Olympic champion Karl Schafer of Austria. Throughout the performances, Maribel and one of the other show headliners grew closer and closer. Before long, the two had fallen deeply in love. Guy Rochon Owen, a former North American Champion in the fours event, was dashing with his slick black hair and slender moustache. He was the consummate showman, often cast in the role of hillbilly

Courtesy of the Winchester Massachusetts Archival Center

Guy Owen and Maribel Vinson in costume together.

or clown, simply because he could pull off those goofball roles so much better than the more serious European skaters. He had even done what Maribel was never able to do—outshine Sonja Henie. A New York newspaper reporter once wrote of Guy, "His sinuous grace and rhythmic fire" had eclipsed Sonja Henie at a benefit performance at Madison Square Garden in 1936.

Guy proposed to Maribel in 1938, and they married soon after. She changed her name legally to Maribel Vinson Owen.

Gay Blades lasted only three years. By now, Sonja Henie had her own hugely successful ice show, the Hollywood Ice Review. It was deemed "the world's biggest box office attraction." Once again, Maribel found herself in direct competition with Sonja Henie, and again, Sonja was winning. By the time Maribel and Guy were married, Sonja was making her fifth Hollywood motion picture. She had become the first female athlete to become a millionaire. Flashbulbs captured Sonja and Hollywood's elite rubbing elbows at movie premieres. She was considered the third biggest box office draw, behind only Shirley Temple and Clark Gable.

Sonja Henie dolls, complete with the famous white skates and tailored dresses, flew off toy store shelves around the world. White boots soon rendered black ones obsolete for women skaters. Cigarette companies inserted Sonja Henie trading cards inside packages. She was featured in magazine and television advertisements. Little girls the world over took up skating so they could be just like Sonja. Maribel was a nine-time U.S. figure skating champion, but she was being beaten in the publicity competition by her archrival—a foreigner who once saluted Hitler. An embarrassing photo of Sonja shaking Hitler's hand after a Berlin performance had emerged, but she was able to deflect the criticism with her usual charm. According to popular legend, she even used the photo to her advantage. Sonja made sure this photo was placed prominently in the foyer of her family's Norwegian estate. When invading Germans came to loot her home, they saw the picture and left the mansion intact. There seemed to be no justice in Sonja's fame.

Maribel's own minor celebrity paled compared to Sonja's. The two women were equally talented in the field of figure skating, but Sonja's physical appearance was much more marketable. Maribel, truth be told, had a large, pointed nose, accentuated by her short, unfeminine hairstyles. To add insult to injury, while Sonja made millions of dollars in groundbreaking Hollywood studio contracts,

Maribel and her new husband struggled to make ends meet in the beginning of their married life.

Guy and Maribel lived wherever the coaching jobs were in supply. First, they took up residence in St. Paul, Minnesota, and then moved to Berkeley, California. Maribel worked hard both as a coach and as a writer during these years. She published the first of her three books about skating, called *Primer*. In California the couple's children were born.

Maribel Yerxa Owen came first. She had the same first and middle name as her mother, their middle names coming from a maternal cousin. To prevent confusion between the mother and daughter, she was called "Mara" or "Little Maribel." Mother was often called "Big Maribel."

Four years later, Laurence Rochon Owen was born. Guy's mother was named Laurence. Laurence had the same middle name as her father. Both girls were on skates, with the help of double runners, by age two.

Maribel continued to write professionally as the family blossomed. In the years after her daughters were born, she produced two more skating books, *Advanced Figure Skating* and *The Fun of Figure Skating.*

Maribel and Guy were opposites in some ways. Maribel was outspoken, and Guy was somewhat shy, according to his former training mates at the Minto Skating Club in Ottawa. Ron Ludington, Maribel's devoted pupil, said that she mentioned Guy occasionally drank too many spirits. Sometimes, the young family would bicker about the rigors of skating. Laurence especially grew tired of the tedium of school figures, and would show reluctance to train. The collective stress of those aspects of life in the Owen home perhaps became too taxing. It appears at some point that Guy and Maribel decided it would be best to separate. In published articles, including the June 1977 issue of *Skating* magazine, Guy was referred to as Maribel's "former" husband.

It appears that Guy moved back to Ottawa, Ontario, to be near his parents. On April 21, 1952, he was stricken with bouts of crushing abdominal pain and rushed to the hospital. He did not survive the night. Some friends say the cause of death was a bleeding ulcer, while others say it was a heart attack. Death records are sealed in Canada to all but immediate family members, and none survive. At the time of his death, Guy was only thirty-nine years old. His obituary in the *Ottawa Citizen* newspaper read:

> OWEN, Guy Rochon—Suddenly in hospital, on Monday, April 21, 1952, Guy Rochon Owen, only and dearly beloved son of Laurence and Arthur Owen. Funeral from Hulse and Playfair Limited, 315 McLeod Street, on Wednesday morning to St. Barnabas Church, for requiem Mass at 10 a.m. Interment, Beechwood Cemetery.

Maribel, Mara, and Laurence were not mentioned in the obituary. It is not known if they left California at any time right before or after Guy's death, or if they attended his funeral Mass.

In a one-column article on page sixteen of the same paper, Guy's competitive record was reported. The article mentioned his two daughters, his parents, an aunt, and his grandparents. For some reason, the fact that he had been married to a nine-time U.S. figure skating champion was not mentioned—a truly conspicuous absence, perhaps by design.

Maribel Vinson Owen was a single mother of two in 1952. That year, her father also passed away, leaving two Vinson widows in a short span of time. Maribel began to age more rapidly, losing the last morsel of gentleness in her face.

Eager to preserve her tough exterior, she never spoke much about Guy's death. She never remarried, and chose to keep his last name. To her closest confidants, she expressed guilt over Guy's demise. In her final skating book, *The Fun of Figure Skating*, published in 1960, she even dedicated the book to "My skating family—mother, father, husband, and daughters who have engendered and sustained my great love of figure skating." This was the first book in which she mentioned ever having a husband—and it came eight years after his death. Ron Ludington said, "Guy had trouble with the fact that Maribel was such a strong person. She took over the male identity. She never remarried and she felt quite guilty about everything that had happened."

Whatever guilt she felt, she buried it in work. Undeterred in her ambitions, she forged ahead in the spirit of family preservation. The Olympic legacy kept her as driven as ever. She took her family back to her hometown of Winchester, Massachusetts, moving in with her mother in the Vinson family's old house on 195 High Street, which they had owned since 1911.

Maribel took a job at the Commonwealth Figure Skating Club eight miles away, but she insisted her daughters skate in the most prestigious club in the country—the Figure Skating Club of Boston. Students said Maribel wanted to work full time for the club and was puzzled that with a record of more U.S. titles than anyone in history, she could be turned down for a full-time coaching job there. Some of her students believed the other coaches didn't like her strong personality and tough coaching tactics. Former student Ron Ludington said, "Maribel pulled a little girl by the ponytail, and the girl fell and broke her wrist. Things were just different then. It was nothing."

The Figure Skating Club of Boston did make one concession: they would allow Maribel to coach her own daughters at the club. This way, Laurence and Little Maribel, who both showed great potential to be champions, would represent the club, enhancing its already glorious reputation. In the first half of the century, almost all of the U.S. champions had come from the Boston Club, which is not surprising, considering there were few year-round indoor rinks in the country. Since the U.S. Nationals event began in 1914, Boston had six ladies champions, many of whom had won multiple titles. Most of the other winners were also from the East Coast—predominately Philadelphia and New York. Boston was also home to the U.S. Figure Skating Association.

In her duties as coach, Maribel taught housewives, dentists, and middle-aged couples looking for a new diversion to their upper-class existence. She coached champions and beginners, the old and the young. In the height of the civil rights movement, she even broke the racial barriers in skating.

Civil rights bills had passed in Congress and were signed into law, but putting those laws into practice seemed a daunting task. The average white American man made $20,000 in these prosperous times. The average black man: only $11,000. By 1947, black players were at last allowed into major league baseball, but figure skating had never seen an elite black skater. Maribel, under her tough exterior, was fighting to make figure skating an equal-opportunity sport.

Maribel would sneak a black girl through the back entrance of the rink and give her lessons for free. The girl, Mabel Fairbanks, had been turned away by the cashier dozens of times. "Colored people aren't allowed in the rink," the cashier would say. Maribel couldn't tolerate this behavior, but didn't want to be fired. And so the lessons took place when the club was closed. Finally, a manager decided to let the persistent little girl into the rink. While Maribel now openly offered lessons to Mabel, others would snicker and stare. Because club membership was denied to blacks, it was impossible for Mabel to compete. She did, however, manage to join some ice revues that played mostly to black audiences. She contacted Sonja Henie about skating in one of her shows, but Sonja declined. Sonja had a history of turning her back on social causes—when the Norwegian Resistance Movement asked her for financial assistance during World War II, she replied that she was now an American citizen and couldn't help them in their fight against Nazi Germany. Mabel went on to coach black students, some of whom eventually competed and won medals in national competitions.

Maribel hated the bigotry she encountered at the skating rinks. According to 1956 Olympic gold medalist Tenley Albright (one of Maribel's former students), Maribel would sometimes pretend she was Jewish in hopes that they'd not express any prejudice in her presence. She was a paradox in this way. At one moment, she could fight for what was right and show heartfelt compassion to a young victim of racism. In other moments, she would swat her students' hindquarters with blade guards, and scold them until they were afraid of her. For this reason, many people *were* afraid of her.

Ron Ludington, however, was not. Ron was one of Maribel's top students, and skated pairs with his wife, Nancy. He was a hard worker but was always ready to crack a joke with his hard New England accent. He sometimes enjoyed testing Maribel's patience, and she respected the fact that he refused to be intimidated by her. Ron and Nancy won a bronze medal at the 1960 Olympics when Maribel was their coach.

One day before the Olympics, Ludington arrived for practice as usual. For some time, he had been carrying around a secret that would surely land him in trouble with Maribel: he had started smoking. He began to warm up before his lessons got underway. He launched into a flying camel spin, and as he spun around in a dizzying blur, his pack of cigarettes flew out of his pocket, and the cigarettes scattered everywhere. One by one, a sheepish Ludington collected the battered and bent cigarettes off the ice surface, inserting them back into the pack. Maribel stood nearby, sporting a deadly glare. She said nothing. She simply stretched out her hand, and into it Ludington silently dropped the pack of cigarettes. He never did get his cigarettes back.

Photo courtesy of Ron Ludington

Ron and Nancy Ludington won a bronze medal under the tutelage of Maribel Vinson Owen at the 1960 Squaw Valley Olympics.

Even though Maribel took on dozens of students, keeping her two daughters in skates was a sizeable expense. She also insisted the girls be well rounded and attend only the best of schools. Mara attended the Girls Latin School in Boston. She joined the Glee and Drama Clubs, played piano, studied ballet, and took tennis lessons. She went on to study sociology and anthropology at Boston

College and aspired to be a teacher. Laurence attended Winchester Academy, where she was known as a "brain." She also played piano and loved modern dance and diving.

Laurence had also inherited one more of her mother's gifts—writing. She wanted to write professionally someday. Laurence was in many ways a carbon copy of her mother. Their talents were the same, their haircuts were alike, and their temperaments could be very similar. Laurence could be energetic and talkative like her mother, but had a soft, quiet side, too. She would often disappear into secret corners where her love of poetry spilled onto the page. Samples of her work survive today.

The Awakening

Softly, Softly the spring comes o'er the tired land
All men awake refreshed;
They rise to greet the world with joy
And birds sing, and all becomes new-born.
Gloom is but a shadow of the night long past;
Hope is the light,
The Radiance.

—Laurence R. Owen

Just before the U.S. National Skating Championships in 1961, Laurence learned she had earned early admittance to the prestigious Radcliffe College, her mother's and grandmother's alma mater. Radcliffe students were now allowed to take classes at Harvard, an opportunity that did not exist for her mother.

As a working mother with four people and dozens of extracurricular activities to support, Vinson Owen took job opportunities wherever they appeared. Every minute of her day was used for some task.

Maribel's gift as a writer landed her a job as a reporter on figure skating for the Associated Press. She was assigned to cover the 1956 Olympics in Cortina, Italy. Though she had worked on the coaching team that guided Tenley Albright, a key contender for a gold medal as the reigning world champion, her new employer ignored this obvious conflict of interest. Tenley had conquered childhood polio to become one of the most beloved sports figures of her time.

She was skating on a badly cut leg, which she had injured in a scary practice incident leading up to her long program. Despite the soreness of her leg, Tenley came through with an inspired performance. In one of the most moving moments in skating history, the audience hummed along to her music. Clapping to the beat is common, but hearing hundreds of voices humming a melody is an unprecedented sign of support. That day, Tenley made history as the first American woman to win an Olympic gold medal in ladies skating. American beauty Carol Heiss took the silver. Maribel didn't have much time to bask in her student's victory; she needed to write about the event for the Associated Press. In her heart, she dreamed of the day one of her daughters would ascend to the gold medal position atop the Olympic podium.

Back in the days before lightning-fast computers, it took a special kind of expertise to understand how to tabulate figure skating results. Victories were often decided by slim tenths of a point, and Maribel possessed a rare understanding of how to determine figure skating scores. One incident affirmed her as the true scoring expert of the day. She had tabulated that Elizabeth Schwartz and Kurt Oppelt of Austria were the winners of the pairs gold medal. Another wire service reported that Canadians Frances Dafoe and Norris Bowman had won the title. Maribel was insistent, but refigured the numbers just to be sure. While the margin of victory was smaller in her second analysis, her stance was the same—the Austrians had won. For two hours, she paced in the hotel office of the Associated Press. After the agonizing wait, the judges announced their results. The Austrian pair had indeed won the gold medal. Maribel, feeling vindicated, "let out a 'whoop' that shook the Alpine peaks," according to coworkers.

Maribel continued writing for the Associated Press for the 1960 Squaw Valley Olympics. This time, her two daughters were competing, another example of how her competing roles as reporter, mother, and coach often collided.

After the ladies compulsory figures had wrapped up, Maribel knelt on the ice, intently focused on the figures traced in the day's competition. Dudley Richards, by now an honorary member of the Owen family, told a nearby reporter, "Mrs. Owen is really hot under the collar. In one of the compulsory figures, five of the nine judges, all Europeans, rated perfectionist Carol Heiss below Sjouhke Dijkstra of Holland. None but Mrs. Owen took the trouble to inspect the marks of the two girls."

Once Maribel left the rink, she blasted the judges. "The marks out there I just inspected prove Carol far ahead of the girl from Holland. Such judging disturbs me. Such judging, or rank ignorance, in judging the all-important compulsory school figures eventually can ruin the sport."

When it was mentioned to Maribel that such remarks about the judging could work against her daughters in the 1961 World Championships in Prague, she said, "Use my name if you think it's the best way to get this judging decline straightened out. I'm not worried about Carol Heiss, David Jenkins, or my daughters, but of the skaters who take over for them in a few years. This sport, especially the judging, must remain sound."

Maribel had harbored her own private resentment over the judging system from her bronze medal at the 1932 Olympics. Now, the pro-European sentiment seemed to be infiltrating yet another Olympic Games.

Maribel's display of anger could cost her the ultimate dream—an Olympic gold medal for her daughters. The high-stakes wheeling and dealing of figure skating judges is well documented. One only needs to point to the 2002 Salt Lake City controversy for proof. French judge Marie Reigne Le Gougne confessed to making an under-the-table deal with Russian judges. In exchange for ranking the Canadian pairs team of Jamie Sale and David Pelletier lower than Russians Elena Berezhnaya and Anton Sikharulidze, the Russian judge would rank the French ice dance team of Marina Annasina and Gwendal Peizerat highest. The plan backfired when the Canadians skated a perfect routine, while the Russians made several mistakes, including botched side-by-side double Axels. The International Olympic Committee, in a first, awarded a second set of gold medals to the Canadians. The French ice dance team won the gold, and the result was never questioned too loudly, as they were considered front-runners anyway.

The most enduring result from the scandal was the complete makeover of the scoring system. By 2005, the World Championships had replaced the old 6.0 scoring system, in favor of assigning credit to each individual element. Maribel surely would have approved and perhaps finally could put to rest her resentment of what she saw as unfair judging in her competition with Sonja Henie.

In reality, Sonja probably never considered Maribel a real threat to her legacy. And yet, though Sonja had won medals and millions, she never quite mastered how to maintain strong, meaningful human relationships. While charitable to many causes, she once sued her own brother in a property dispute. He coauthored a book about some of Sonja's many flaws and tirades. Sonja had two messy divorces, and never had children. Her own countrymen were still at odds with her over her perceived friendliness with Hitler. Nevertheless, she somehow managed to be adored by the public. Maribel, however, won many victories that Sonja couldn't match. She may not have enjoyed the same level of public adulation, but she had something much more important and enduring—the love of her two daughters. A passion for skating fortified their bond, and gave Maribel a chance to renew her legacy through their future successes.

That road to glory seemed to begin in 1961. Tragedy in the Owen family had at last yielded itself to the promise that the Nationals held for these strong and complex women. At the Broadmoor Ice Palace, they, along with Dudley, walked around as a pack, never separating for too long. Laurence began her warm-up stretches under her mother's discerning gaze. Somehow, Laurence managed to maintain her smile as she stretched. She was careful not to overwork her injured knee, aware that one wrong move could end the dream. A nervous glance at the clock revealed that the time to lace her skates had arrived. Laurence carefully pulled her freshly polished skates out of her traveling bag, and began loosening the laces to make way for her stocking-clad feet. First, her right foot, then her left—she never varied from this routine. She jammed each skate into the floor to make sure her heels were properly situated in the part of the skate called the "heel cup." The intricate work of lacing the skate to the proper tightness began. Most skaters know that skates can be temperamental, fitting differently from day to day. In the superstitious mind of a competitive athlete, an odd fit can nag at one's concentration. Laurence, satisfied she had managed a passable job lacing the boots to their usual feel, stood, tugged at her skating dress, and shook out her legs. She began the walk to the side of the rink with her mother by her side. Mara and Dudley offered hugs of luck before heading for the grandstands.

Mother and daughter, though surrounded by other skaters, coaches, and impatient ice monitors, still somehow managed to feel alone, isolated in a universe to which only they could retreat—an exclusive place where a champion looked at her daughter and saw herself staring back.

Chapter Five

"Skate just like you did in practice." Mother Maribel's parting words, uttered in her famous gravelly voice to Laurence, considered a favorite for a national championship. "Don't forget to breathe, relax, and above all, have fun."

"I'm ready," a determined Laurence said, briefly replacing her radiant smile with pinched lips and an intense glare. She took a controlled deep breath to calm her racing heart and settle her nerves. In 1960, Laurence was still a somewhat unknown skater, taking part in her first full year of international competition. This year, she was the heir apparent to the American skating crown, attracting attention that could be gratifying in one instant and intimidating the next.

On that Thursday morning, as Laurence waited for the announcer to signal the start of the nerve-wracking compulsory figures portion of the competition, Steffi Westerfeld and coach Edi Scholdan stood just a few feet away. Steffi was as still as a mannequin, eyes shut as she mentally visualized her moves.

"Keep moving," Edi said with his strong German-Austrian accent. "Don't freeze up." Steffi snapped out of her trance and began to walk, shaking out her arms and ankles from time to time to keep her body loose.

Myra and Sherri sat in the arena's newly installed wooden seats, inching closer to the edge with each passing moment. When the time came to begin, Myra clutched her handkerchief tightly in her gloved hands. She appeared more nervous than Steffi, painfully aware that at this point, there was nothing she could do to help her daughter. Sherri, always the calming influence, cupped her hands over her mother's. They both exhaled, their breath visible in the chilly air.

The stadium fell silent as the five judges, led by a referee, carefully scooted across the ice, clipboards and pencils in hand. Maribel's hands reached out and grasped Laurence's hands and, as mother and coach, she looked her daughter squarely in the eyes and uttered one last encouragement.

"You can do this. Don't be nervous."

The ladies lined up waiting for the door to the ice surface to swing open. Judging by their expressions, they looked as if they were being led to the executioner. Skating judges can be a stern bunch, and nothing makes one feel more vulnerable than being judged. At last, the door creaked open and the skaters were ushered onto the ice, their blades scraping to a stop as they reached their starting positions.

The school figures were divided up so skaters wouldn't have to do them all at once. The maneuvers were notoriously taxing on the ankles, and this system allowed a little stretching in between moves.

Skaters were individually summoned to the judges standing on the ice. One by one, the referee called out the names of the figures. Circle eight. Serpentine. Double three. Paragraph Loop. These names, all but foreign to skaters starting out today, were worth sixty percent of the score in 1961.

The tone of the competition was set early. A seesaw battle between Laurence and Steffi soon emerged. The scores were announced after each set of figures. Naturally, the easiest figures came first. Round one went to Laurence. Then Steffi took the lead. Laurence took it back. They watched each other, and even though they were engaged in the most important competition of their lives, they congratulated each other sincerely at the successful completion of each move. The final set of figures was the most difficult, and Laurence struggled with at least a few of these in practice. Mentally, she drifted back in time to 1956, when she fell doing a compulsory figure during the National Junior Championships and broke her wrist. This time, she completed the difficult figures better than she ever had done them before. Steffi breezed through too, seeming to relax more and more with each element. Maribel, who literally wrote the book on how to perform figures, looked worried on the sidelines. She was incapable of hiding her emotions. Laurence skated to her mother, Mara, and Dudley, and seemed to know by her mother's expression that first place would be unlikely. The total marks for school figures were announced, and as expected, Steffi had claimed a slight lead.

Myra and Sherri rushed to embrace Steffi, and a quiet celebration ensued. "I just have to get through the free skate," Steffi said, her voice containing a mixture of relief and anxiety. She would have to perform disastrously to walk away without a medal at all. The gold medal was hers, at least for the moment. The free skate, worth forty percent of the score, was scheduled for Friday night. Edi, like most coaches, never celebrated anything until the event was over. He reviewed with Steffi what figures she should work on before the North American Championships just three weeks away.

Nearby, Maribel instructed, "You have to do a nice free skate, Laurence. And the Westerfeld girl will hopefully make some mistakes."

The more than twenty-four hours of waiting seemed like an eternity. Maribel's focus would be split Friday, too, as Mara's and Dudley's crucial pairs event was also scheduled for Friday night.

Courtesy of the Winchester Massachusetts Archival Center

Dudley Richards and Maribel formed a romance, according to friends.

Though winning a ladies title was much more prestigious, the pairs event was gaining in popularity. Mara and Dudley were practically shoe-ins for the gold, in that they had won a silver medal the year before, and the 1960 gold medalists had retired.

During their three-year on-ice partnership, something beautiful had blossomed between Mara and Dudley. She was only a teenager when they first became partners, and he was a man of twenty-six. The age difference was hardly acceptable to forge a relationship in the beginning, but when she came of age, Dudley's attraction to her was undeniable.

Called "Dud" by his closest friends and family, his was a life of privilege. He grew up near the Kennedy family compound in Hyannisport, Massachusetts, and spent many a sun-soaked day on the Cape, sailing with Jack, Bobby, and Teddy Kennedy. Dud fit in well with the Kennedy clan, famous for their highly competitive touch football games and Herculean ambitions.

Ted Kennedy reminisces fondly about his dear friend:"Dudley had an excellent discipline about him, getting up at 4:30 a.m. for practice. He was just tireless and dedicated."

Young Teddy and Bobby used to sail against Dud and his brother Ross. One outing at the pier nearly ended Dudley's skating career. Kennedy recalled, "He dove off the boat into the pier and injured his neck. That put him in a cast. It got him off skating for a year when he was seventeen years old."

Dudley fought back from the injury with the tenacity and unconquerable spirit for which he was so well known. A year after the injury, Dud returned to the ice, and was jumping almost right away. He and Tenley Albright soon partnered and won the 1951 Eastern Sectional Championships. The partnership did not last long.

Tenley said while running through a program once, "Dud hit a rut during a toss, then I was knocked out. Father put his foot down and told us to stick to singles skating."

Dud won the bronze medal as a singles skater at the 1953 U.S. Nationals, and placed as high as fifth at Worlds. His true preference was pairs, and in 1954, he won a sectional medal again with partner Anita Andres. That same year, he graduated from Harvard. While there, he shared a room with his friend Teddy Kennedy. The school awarded Dud a special Major "H" for non-college sports, an honor previously only given to two-time Olympic gold medal skater Dick Button and golf legend Bobby Jones. After college, Dud did what many young men of the time were expected to do when family honor was deemed important—he joined the Army and served for two years.

When he had completed his Army service, he wanted to get back into skating. Today, you wouldn't expect an Army private to be terribly interested in figure skating. Skating certainly didn't have the flamboyance it does now. It was more like a ballroom dance for dapper gentlemen. The men wore proper dress clothes—suited more for church, or even a dinner party, than a physically demanding workout. Even some of Hollywood's most macho leading men, such as Tyrone Powers, sported figure skates for screen roles with Sonja Henie. In these film roles, romance, wealth, and ice were inextricably linked.

Upon his return from Army service, Dud skated some sessions at the Figure Skating Club of Boston, and he caught the eye of Big Maribel. It just so happened that she needed a new pairs partner for Little Maribel. With partner Chuck Foster, Mara had claimed the 1955 U.S. title in the junior pairs division, and a bronze medal in the senior Nationals in 1956. Her skating career seemed on course but then came the devastating blow.

Chuck announced he was leaving the sport. "We had skated together for three years," Foster remembered. "I was twenty, and Little Maribel was fifteen. I graduated from Harvard, and in those days, you got on with your life. There were very few opportunities to make a living skating professionally."

Foster wanted to study medicine. He recalled his news was not received well by Mara and her mother. He went to their house and asked them to sit down before announcing, "I wanted you to know I am quitting to pursue a career in medicine."

"What!" exploded Maribel. "But you made the world team! You can't leave now!"

Mara cried and watched hopelessly as her mother tried to convince Chuck to continue training at least until Worlds was over, but their begging did not change his mind.

Chuck eventually abandoned his medical studies in exchange for the lucrative wholesale lumber business. He never completely abandoned skating, though. He frequently judged events, and was elected president of the USFSA in 2003. That year he was also inducted into the World Skating Hall of Fame.

Mara went several months without a partner when Dudley showed up at the rink again. At the time, Dud had just started work at a real estate firm, and was even appointed to the United States Figure Skating Association Executive Committee. He was handsome and accomplished. It certainly wasn't unusual for a twenty-six-year-old to still be competitively skating, but most people assumed that with his extensive competitive record, he'd want to retire from the sport. Dud, though, hadn't fulfilled his championship desires. He had skated since he was nine years old and had never made an Olympic team. The highlight of his career was winning a junior championship.

Mara had invested years in pairs skating and found her career very much in limbo when Chuck left for school. She felt abandoned and hurt. If a skater loses a pairs partner, it has career-ending potential. Most pairs skaters haven't mastered all of the demanding elements of singles skating, so taking up a new discipline and succeeding is unlikely.

Two partnerless pairs skaters were practicing at the Figure Skating Club of Boston. One day Maribel glided up to Dud, probably without even consulting her daughter.

"Excuse me. Dudley Richards, right?"

"Yes, ma'am."

"You and my daughter have something in common."

"What's that?"

"You both need pairs partners. She's standing right over there. How about giving her a spin?"

Dudley, at 5'10" compared to Mara's 5'6", was a perfect partner for Mara. Their skating levels were comparable. Talk of competing nationally began almost immediately, and Dudley was ready to pursue a championship again.

At first, Maribel would only let them do crossovers around the ice—the most basic kind of stroking. "You must learn each others' rhythm and timing," she said. Next, they began their side-by-side spin combinations. Even some of the world's elite pairs today struggle with the unison of their spins. One skater of the two must count off the revolutions so both skaters know when to rise up and complete the move.

Next, the side-by-side jumps. They both knew the jumps, but needed to develop the right timing. In 1961, there were no throw jumps, by far one of the most dangerous and dazzling elements of skating today. Couples on the world scene now are performing throw triples—some of the Chinese pairs are even trying throw quadruple Salchows—but these moves did not exist in 1961. The other gravity-defying element crucial to present-day skating success—one that makes it unarguably one of the most dangerous sports—was strictly forbidden in 1961. The overhead lift can simulate flight like no other move in skating. It can also create some of the loudest gasps from the audience.

In 2004, audiences were stunned when reigning world champions Tatiana Totmianina and Maxim Marinin of Russia, while performing an overhead lift, suffered a horrifying accident. Maxim's foot appeared to slip from beneath him, and Tatiana hit the ice—head first, at full throttle. A hush fell over the 26,000 people in the audience. Their coach, Olympic champion Oleg Vasiliev, slid in his dress shoes across the ice and signaled with his hand for the referee to cut the music. Tatiana lay motionless on the ice for a few minutes before paramedics put her on a stretcher and took her to the hospital. Remarkably, she suffered no lingering effects, and in 2005, the couple won their second consecutive world championship.

Instead of overhead lifts, Mara and Dud would perform something called a "lasso lift," where Dud would lift Mara in one continuous motion just under his shoulders, and she would do a half a turn in the air and land. The USFSA rulebook prohibited any kind of "hovering" in the air.

Mara and Dud approached skating as strictly business when they first joined forces. The bond that skating creates, however, is irrepressible. The trust involved, the mutual touching, and the shared joys and defeats have spawned many romances. No greater romance exists in skating, though, than the great love affair between Ekaterina Gordeeva and Sergei Grinkov, two-time Olympic gold medalists. She was just a scrawny child when the powerful Soviet skating system paired her with Sergei. Katia bloomed into a beautiful woman right before the world's eyes, and then the romantic sparks flew. The two were married and had a child. They showcased their love for each other in every skating performance. In the midst of highly athletic routines, their love glowed. Their final poses always lingered for an extra moment, as Sergei held her close, their lips nearly touching, creating a sensational tension for everyone in the audience. The skating world's collective heart broke when Sergei died suddenly in 1995. At age twenty-eight, he had a heart attack, likely from an inherited cardiac defect. Katia's love story became a television special and a best-selling book and launched pairs skating into the spotlight.

As Mara came of age in the partnership, Dud began to notice how she had gone from a pretty teenager to a beautiful young woman. Her beauty did not bring her happiness, though. Mara, in a household of strict demands and an unrelenting schedule of college and skating, began to feel a great deal of stress. She took after her father in both appearance and demeanor. She, like her fragile father, developed a bleeding ulcer. Her weight kept dropping lower and lower. She was given medicine, but continued skating and studying through the pain.

Dudley found himself wanting simply to take care of her. He was gentle to her in practice. If she fell, he rushed over to extend his hand. Big Maribel had come to understand that Dudley was a boyfriend, brother, and father figure all rolled into one—a combination that Mara desperately needed.

Girls in these days were expected to marry right out of college. With Mara's senior year nearly complete, Dud was prepared to ask for her hand in marriage. In a family where identity was forever linked with the family legacy, a marriage to Dud could bring Mara something she craved—her own identity, a last name different from her mother—the chance to be "Dudley's wife" instead of "Maribel's daughter" or "Laurence's big sister." The thought was intoxicating. Close friends say Dud planned to propose at the World Championships in Prague. The key to that plan, of course, was winning at the Nationals.

Friday was the day of reckoning for Laurence, Mara, Dud, Steffi Westerfeld, and all the others who had made it this far. Before the ladies and pairs competition got underway on that day, some of the novice and junior level preliminary rounds took place. Skating has a stepladder system. To compete at a certain level, tests must be passed. Novice skaters next aspire to pass their junior tests and junior-level skaters work toward their senior tests.

In modern competitions, the senior ladies free-skating event is always saved for last. Savvy television producers know this is the event that will draw the most attention as America's new ice queen is crowned. In 1961, however, the ladies came first in the final four senior disciplines. The five women with the highest marks skated last. This group is often called "the final flight." Laurence, Steffi, Rhode Michelson, Karen Howland, and Victoria Fisher made up that flight and went out for their warm-up. The main difference between skating then and skating now is that instead of loading routines with triple jumps, ladies performed double jumps.

The pre-competition warm-ups can be beneficial in properly stretching and building confidence, but they can also be dastardly in that some skaters may tire themselves in an effort to look impressive right out of the gate. There is, too, the inherent risk of collision. The most skilled singles skaters become quite adept at avoiding each other, almost as if they have developed well-trained eyes in the back of their heads. Sometimes, a bit of gamesmanship comes into play at these warm-up sessions. At the 2002 U.S. Nationals, quite a buzz surrounded the odd events of the senior ladies warm up. Michelle Kwan, reigning champion and clear favorite, found herself constantly tripping over up-and-coming world contender Sasha Cohen. Sasha, though delicate in appearance, is known as a fierce competitor and perfectionist. Throughout the warm-up period, Sasha had an uncanny knack for needing the same patch of ice as Michelle. Newspaper photographers caught several of these moments on film. Figure skating columnist Christine Brennan of *USA Today* (and also an *ABC Wide World of Sports* commentator) accused Sasha of unsportsmanlike conduct. Sasha denied she was skating into Michelle on purpose, but Michelle handily won the public relations war in this instance, as well as the championship itself.

Legendary two-time Olympic gold medalist Katarina Witt, on the other hand, was quite open about admitting her demonstrations of gamesmanship. She would watch other skaters run their routines, instantly memorize their choreography, and perform the exact routine step for step, much to the simultaneous amazement and irritation of the other competitors. French skater Surya Bonaly, feeling a bit chafed that another skater got in her way in a pre-Olympic warm up, performed a back flip right in front of the offending skater. Back flips are illegal in amateur skating competition, and the referee issued a stern warning.

In 1961, the ladies did indeed behave like ladies and there were no demonstrations of poor behavior, unseemly glares, or gamely gestures. Coaches took their place at the sidelines analyzing every move, careful to offer suggestions that would not create self-doubt, but perhaps boost their skater's performance even slightly. Warm-ups usually start with skaters just moving around in circles. About thirty seconds of that, and the jumps began launching. Audience members cheered when their favorites landed successfully. The warm-up became its own competition to see who garnered the most cheers.

The announcer's voice finally rang out in a dull monotone—"There is one minute remaining in the warm-up."—but the manner of the announcement did not dim the suspense in the arena. Suddenly, all the competitors picked up the pace of their practice, as full panic seemed to set in. The moment had arrived.

"The warm-up has ended," the announcer intoned. "Skaters, please clear the ice."

The competitors had skated their programs numerous times and could do them in their sleep. On their home ice surfaces, they played their music and relied on other skaters to obey the customary etiquette of yielding to a skater doing a program. In some rinks, the skater playing his or her music must wear a sash. Only rarely does the time come when a skater has the luxury of private ice. When the moment to compete arrives, singles skaters are at their most vulnerable. They stand alone in what at times feels like a fishbowl. In 1961, the pressure-packed event must have been even more intimidating by the presence of television cameras, and the knowledge that these cameras would reveal every bit of beauty, and every bit of sloppiness, to the whole country.

Those cameras would also reveal one of the main differences between skating then and now—the size of the skaters. Today's top skaters are all tiny and lean. To complete the revolutions in the triple jumps now being performed, skaters have to maintain a low body weight. Tonya Harding, for example, was the first American woman to complete a triple Axel, but when she started to put on weight, she lost the very jump that made her famous. In the broadcast from 1961, it's easy to see that the skaters were larger.

They had womanly curves. They were not too thin, nor were they sculpted. Overall, the skaters were taller back then, too. Laurence, for example, was 5'6" and easily a size eight. Today's emphasis on being super thin was not a concern at all in 1961.

Obeying the announcer's call to clear the ice, the skaters ended their warm-ups and headed off the rink. As a fitting climax, Steffi and Laurence were slated to be the last two ladies to skate. Steffi had a few crucial advantages—her acclimation to the mountain air (Colorado Springs rests at 6,000 feet), and her knowledge of every subtlety of the Broadmoor Arena.

Following the school figures, a battle for the bronze had erupted between Karen Howland, Rhode Michelson, and Vicky Fisher. Rhode, a Californian, was fifth in the school figures. She came from a skating family, which included a brother who was a national speed skating champion. Rhode herself had taken some speed skating lessons for a time. Both of her parents worked to pay for her skating, and Rhode would skate six hours a day, with no parents on the sidelines to support her. The rink was lonely, with the exception of the little girls who idolized her and always tugged on her skating skirt for attention.

When she stroked onto the ice for her free skate, it became obvious why her figures were not terribly strong. Rhode, a fiery brunette with large, defined muscles and an hourglass figure, clearly spent the bulk of her practices working on jumps. She performed jumps as high as the men were doing, and skated just as quickly as the men, too. Her landings were never in doubt. Her spins were blazing fast. Rhode did seem to tire at the end of her program, and she put her second foot down on a jump or two, but overall, her skills in the jumps and spins were among the strongest. She earned higher marks than the other two girls vying for the bronze and secured a spot on the podium.

Skating, however, is not just about the jumping. In France, it's called "Patinage Artistique," which means "artistic skating." The truly magical skaters are the ones who combine grace and athleticism. Rhode still had some artistic maturing to do, but at only seventeen, she still had time. If one were to compare her style to a modern skater, the muscular Tonya Harding and Japan's Midori Ito come to mind. Their artistry never fully developed, even as they won championships in national and international competitions. Rhode's jumps were solid, but she just needed to nurture her softer side. With the 1964 Olympics still three years away, she had time to put all the pieces together.

Steffi was up next. She was almost assured a medal—but it wasn't yet decided which color the medal would be. She sat atop the standings, but only by a slim margin. Her name was called in the same drab way the others had been announced.

"Representing the Broadmoor Figure Skating Club, please welcome Stephanie Westerfeld."

The third syllable of her last name was drowned out by excited applause, whistling, and the stomping of feet. Her long-sleeved dress sparkled with dozens of perfectly placed rhinestones that were set ablaze by the bright bulbs lighting the arena.

When Steffi reached her starting position, the crowd stilled to silence. She sported a forced smile and stretched her arms wide, like a lovely bird ready to take flight. With that first pose, she presented a striking contrast to Rhode Michelson. Steffi was elegant down to the pointed position of her fingers, her wrists flexed upward in the classic style of a prima ballerina. She took a final breath before her music began, and almost right away, the silky fabric of her family's dreams unraveled.

Her first element, a single Axel, was strong and secure. Her second jump, however, was a double Axel, the most difficult jump being performed by the ladies in 1961, and she "cheated" the jump. This means she landed it on one foot but didn't execute the full two-

and-a-half revolutions required. Her second double Axel was also severely under-rotated. Her double flip was not much more successful. She "popped" this jump, meaning that midair, her body opened up and did not squeeze in tightly enough for two revolutions.

She regained her composure midway through her program. Her double Salchow and spread eagles (a move with a decidedly unfortunate name, but the quintessential show-stopping move,) were perfect. Her footwork sequence was delicate, if not a little watered-down in its simplicity, and her double toe loop was a success. She attempted one more double—a loop, which can be a frightening jump. To perform this move, skaters must move backward, and bend into the deepest part of the blade's back outside edge. This jump creates a sensation of leaning backward. When Steffi attempted it, the problem began on the takeoff, when she simply didn't show any conviction by truly "snapping" her body into the jump. The result barely looked like a single jump—she landed so severely on her toe pick that she had to hop to regain her balance. One of her last jumps was a single Lutz. In Sonja's and Maribel's day, a single Lutz was truly an amazing spectacle. By 1961, single jumps were passé—considered quite easy, in fact.

Steffi's music ended, and she politely bowed to the judges and the audience, her smile failing to conceal the bitter disappointment she felt with herself. Myra and Sherri walked down to the side of the rink to greet a still breathless Steffi, and do everything they could to assure her she was still going to win a medal. Depending on what Laurence would do, Steffi still had a gold medal in her sights, but felt it slipping away.

Laurence was announced and the crowd warmly welcomed her. Maribel stood by to remind Laurence, "The door is wide open. The gold is yours for the taking."

Laurence's face erupted into a beaming smile as she skated onto the ice. Other girls had elected to wear very ordinary costumes, but Laurence wore a dress with loose, draped layers of fabric that highlighted her individual and somewhat modern taste. Her short bangs fluttered in the breeze created by her speed as she raced to her starting position before skidding to a stop. She arrived at center ice, made a few nervous adjustments to her footing, and then exhaled forcefully. A sudden peace seemed to come upon her as she waited for the first beat of the music.

With that first beat, Laurence began skating, bringing the audience along in a kind of rapture. She opened with some quick footwork, and the music started to build in intensity. She performed a jump sequence, not to be confused with a combination jump. Combinations require two jumps back-to-back without any steps in between. A jump sequence allows skaters to insert steps between jumps to gain speed or balance. Today, triple-triple combinations are the notorious thorn in Michelle Kwan's side. The absence of them is suspected of costing her two Olympic gold medals—one to Tara Lipinski, and the other to Sarah Hughes.

Laurence's jump sequence consisted of a waltz jump (half a revolution), an Axel, and an Axel straight into a sit spin. Her skating routine consisted of a considerable amount of dance. Her arms were always fluid—placed with the mood of the music in mind.

She successfully executed her double Salchow, double loop, and camel spin. Normal program fatigue, or perhaps the altitude, began to show when she slightly under-rotated a double flip jump. Laurence, like Steffi, also planned the treacherous double Axel jump. Her version of the jump was also slightly cheated but had better air position than Steffi's, with her "free leg," (the opposite of the "landing leg,") perfectly crossed over the other.

Laurence performed a more difficult routine than Steffi's, even attempting a double Lutz. This jump, considered one of the hardest, was landed on two feet and with a slight forward lean. A layback spin, one of the most dramatic and beautiful moves in all

Photo courtesy of Bob McIntyre

The 1961 U.S. Ladies Nationals medalists from left: Rhode Michelson, Laurence Owen, and Steffi Westerfeld.

of skating, came next, and Laurence created a textbook photo of a truly well-done layback.

Her speed continued to build. Her smile continued to widen. Following the last major element—a high-flying split jump—Laurence seemed to know she was in the home stretch. Her routine wasn't technically perfect, but there was something magical and magnetic about it. She interpreted the music, instead of treating it as merely background noise. Her final move was a cross-foot spin, which was perfectly centered and turned Laurence into a blur before everyone's eyes. When the spin came to a stop, she threw her arms into the air and tilted her neck up, her smile reaching to the top of the stands.

Laurence took her time bowing, unlike other competitors who seemed to hurry off the ice. Once her bows were complete, she dashed over to the sidelines, where her sister and mother rushed to embrace her. They bounced up and down as they hugged. Even before the scores were announced, Laurence pranced back onto the ice to bow once again, and the audience obliged her with more enthusiastic applause. When the scores came up (ranging from 5.5 to 5.8), they confirmed what Laurence already seemed to know in her heart—that she was the champion. She was the first competitor ever to win the same title as her or his parent.

It can be said that Steffi lost the championship more than Laurence had won it. Her nerves, the hometown pressure, the family strife—it all may have finally overpowered Steffi. One judge still ranked Steffi first. The most perplexing judging of all concerned Rhode Michelson, who was ranked fifth in the free skate by one of the judges. Rhode clearly was second only to Laurence in this portion of the competition.

Rather than emphasize the loss, Steffi instead turned her spirits around by focusing on the fact that she had accomplished a first for her family—a medal at the U.S. Nationals. She saw the Owen party celebrating in the lobby and tapped on Laurence's shoulder. The two simultaneously clasped each other in a sincere embrace. While they may have established a rivalry on the ice, the two girls struggled to dislike each other. Both girls were so *nice*. Their hearts had no room for ugliness. Their names would be forever linked on the ladies podium:

Gold: Laurence Owen

Silver: Stephanie Westerfeld

Bronze: Rhode Michelson

Celebrations were cut short by Maribel, ever the taskmaster, who had more pupils to ready for the evening's competition. If Mara and Dud could win, Maribel would be one of three champions living under one roof.

Chapter Six

The customary ten-minute warm-ups before the final free skate in the pairs division were done with a fair amount of caution. Anyone who has seen a pairs event understands that the most tense moments on the ice, at least from an audience member's perspective, are these warm-ups. It's much more difficult for two people to get out of someone's path than only one. Teams eager to squeak out every element before the final free skate sometimes become so focused on the moves that they can come dangerously close to colliding. It happened at the 2002 Olympics. Eventual dual gold medal teams Jamie Sale and David Pelletier of Canada and Elena Berezhnaya and Anton Sikharulidze of Russian slammed into each other while doing simple backward skating. Anton and Jamie seemed to bear the biggest brunt of the impact, as Anton sat on the ice, shaken, and Jamie somehow prevented herself from hitting the ice, but doubled over, grasping her abdomen. Minutes later, they were all expected to regain their composure and skate at the biggest event of their lives.

The 1961 pairs warm-up passed with no injuries, and no terribly close calls. Mara and Dud drew a lower number in the starting order, so they had time to recover from the practice and listen to Maribel's last-minute instruction. They seemed extremely relaxed, even affectionate with each other before their skate. They were, after all, favorites. But something happened that nearly ended their championship hopes before they even took the ice. Dud's blade started to break off his boot. The blades are screwed into the boot leather, but because he had tightened the blades so many times, the screw was getting worn and had lost its bite. The blade was wobbling and not at all secure. Maribel rushed around trying to find a temporary repair kit. Maintenance crews in the rink were able to scrounge up a screw and screwdriver that would make the necessary repairs. Dudley was still trying to wiggle the blade just before their names were called. If this had happened in practice, Maribel would very likely have scolded Dud for not purchasing a new pair of skates. He had been wearing these for five years, too long for an elite skater. Mara and Dud relied on their competitive experience and meticulous practice sessions to carry them through the scare.

Dud was the most experienced competitor at the 1961 U.S. Nationals. At age twenty-nine, he had been competing for twenty years. Some of his fellow pairs competitors were half his age. Those youngsters went first.

Ila (pronounced EYE-lah) Ray Hadley, eighteen, and Ray Hadley, seventeen, the dark-haired brother-and-sister team from Seattle, took to the ice first for their long program. From the time they were born, their father, Ray, knew he would have them in skates. Actually, they began with roller skating. Ray was a former champion roller skater. He was also a dreamer, and one of his dreams dictated that his children would be Olympic figure skating champions, modeled after the success of Seattle skaters Karol and Peter Kennedy, who won a silver medal in the Olympics in 1952 in the pairs event. Ray's second wife, Alvah "Linda" Hadley, was a professional figure skater who made the perfect partner in attaining those dreams of Olympic glory. She served in the dual role of stepmother and coach.

By the time they were ten years old, Ray and Ila Ray showed enormous promise. Their father was often annoyed at how difficult it was for his star children to find ice time to practice their elements with enough repetition. Ray began drawing up plans for his ultimate dream—a skating studio where his children could have as much time as they needed to practice. Eleven years after first hatching this idea, the Hadley and Hart Skating Studio opened, with half of the name taken from Linda's professional skating name, Linda Hart. Four hundred people attended the open house for the new studio, which at the time, was the largest privately owned ice rink in the country. The studio contained 4,800 square feet of ice, with mirrors lining the sides in the traditional ballet-studio setup.

Both Ila Ray and Ray were focused competitors. Ila Ray, a wavy-haired brunette, was known for being the more fiery one of the pair—a perfectionist who was about to begin classes at the University of Washington in hopes of a teaching career. Ray was a blue-eyed brunette who was extremely popular with the girls and was also a natural-born leader, as president of his senior class. He planned to become either a lawyer or a businessman someday.

Both of the Hadleys had a light sense of humor off the ice, but on the ice, they were disciplined and driven. They were very clear in stating that they intended to make the 1964 Olympic Team but were still quite modest; they easily became embarrassed about all the attention they received. Nothing could pull them away from that Olympic dream—even when a terrible fall cut a large gash in Ila Ray's calf, a gash that required twenty-four stitches. Four days later, she was back on the ice, training for the Olympic dream. The Seattle siblings were extremely pleased when that Olympic dream came four years earlier than expected.

After winning important regional events, they won the bronze

Photo courtesy of the Seattle Figure Skating Club

Ila Ray and Ray Hadley.

medal at the 1960 U.S. Nationals, earning a spot on the Squaw Valley Olympic team. When they arrived in Squaw Valley that cold February, everything that could go wrong did. The energy dripped out of them, their bodies ached, and their heads pounded. In the biggest moment of their lives, they came down with the flu.

Instead of feeling bad about their predicament, they did not miss a single practice session leading up to the event. Practices went smoothly. But the evening of the free skate, their dream took a nightmarish turn. Skating at full tilt, the Hadleys crashed into the legendary Russian pairs team Oleg Protopopov and Ludmilla Belousova. Audience members gasped as the four skaters were strewn on the surface like tossed dice. The teams had only a few minutes left in the warm-up and had very little time to mentally and physically recover. Ila Ray took a nasty spill in their long program. They ended up placing eleventh. They knew they needed to try the Olympics one more time so they could skate their best in front of the world. This dream-chasing would put a severe dent on the family finances. Drowning in loan payments for the Hadley-Hart Ice Studio, Mr. Hadley had virtually no hard cash to pay for travel and equipment. The Seattle community pitched in to help with expenses.

In 1961, they were the only real threat to Mara's and Dud's championship hopes. Just seconds after Ray and Ila Ray glided to the center point of the rink, the polite applause dimmed, and music blared through the speakers. The Hadleys skated to the music "I Could Have Danced All Night," from the motion picture *My Fair Lady*. On the ice, they didn't fill their routine with any extraneous arm movements or dramatic choreography. They took their time setting up for each element, which at times seemed cautious but resulted in a precision that meant no visible mistakes. Five minutes later, they had completed a conservative, but successful program. In both sets of marks, the Hadleys earned between 4.9 and 5.6 out of a possible six.

Mara and Dud were next. They held hands as they skated to their starting position, she in a fur-trimmed costume, and he in an ascot, sport jacket, and dinner slacks. As soon as the music started, they sprung into action and accomplished what great athletes often do—they made it look easy.

The broken blade and ensuing nerves by now seemed a distant memory, but Dudley did nearly take a spill during some very slow, easy footwork. Fortunately, the mistake looked like just a small balance check, and didn't seem to faze them. Technically, this was the kind of program one would call "clean"—no mistakes or huge disruptions. The judges held up their tall, white score cards. Their marks ranged from 5.5-5.8, which confirmed Mara and Dud had taken the lead.

Only one medal-contending pair remained. William Holmes Hickox and Laurie Jean Hickox were the children of Lute and

Elinor Hickox of Berkeley, California. Laurie was adopted, but the two were just as close as natural siblings. Skating was just one of the many talents the children possessed.

Bill was a percussionist with his school marching band, a talent that earned him a trip to the opening ceremonies of the Squaw Valley Olympics. Bill also enjoyed photography and Scottish dancing. The six-foot-tall redhead was aiming toward a career in science. Laurie was a dark brunette with porcelain skin, who was a gifted ballerina and baton twirler. She also spoke Spanish and enjoyed modern dancing.

Laurie and Bill had skated pairs together for years as members of the Skating Club of San Francisco, where Maribel was their first instructor. Bill was only seven and Laurie just four. In 1959, they won the U.S. Junior Pairs title. When Bill turned seventeen, he started to look beyond skating and to the military for his future. He gained acceptance to the Air Force Academy in Colorado Springs, leaving Laurie without a partner. She began to train as a singles skater but found the transition difficult and frustrating. Though she had a good chance at making an Olympic team as a pairs skater, she was too far beyond her prime to take up singles with any real hope of becoming a champion.

The family made the decision to send Laurie to Colorado Springs so she could train with her brother again. Too much of their lives had been invested in skating to just throw it all away, they thought. Edi Scholdan took them as pupils. They soon regained their form and were winning important regional competitions, as they looked toward the 1964 Olympics. Then, in November, 1960, duty once again interfered. Bill was asked to march at the inauguration of John F. Kennedy on January 25, 1961. If he went to Washington, he would miss Nationals. The whole Hickox family waited for Bill to make his decision: skating, or the President. More pointedly, the choice came between breaking his sister's heart and serving the President. Bill decided duty to family was more important in this case. The military officially excused him from his inaugural duties so he could compete.

Bill and Laurie managed to skate well enough for some respectable marks, but they clearly lacked some of the difficulty and artistry of the other teams. Mara and Dud retained their lead, and the second history-making moment of the night was achieved—Mara had won the same pairs title won by her mother more than twenty years earlier.

Mara and Dud embraced, only to be interrupted by Maribel and Laurence who piled in for a group hug. Through all the tears, tragedies, fights, and illness, this moment washed away the bitter taste of those struggles. This had been a night of perfection for the Owen family.

Still, Maribel couldn't resist the temptation to offer her opinion about the results. Jim Browning and Janet Browning, a husband-and-wife pairs team from Indianapolis, placed fifth. She told Jim Browning, "You got robbed. You should have been third."

Instead, on the pairs podium were:

Gold: Dudley Richards and Maribel Y. Owen

Silver: Ray and Ila Ray Hadley

Bronze: William and Laurie Hickox

Browning and his wife expected to be named as alternates to the team, but in a surprise move, the skating association named the junior couple from Chicago as the first alternates, instead of the Brownings. It just so happened the deciding judge was from Chicago.

More championships had to be decided, and those events would be held on Saturday. The Owens, the toast of the event, could now roam freely as spectators with not a worry in the world. Laurence had lived up to her mother's reputation. Now, Laurence was being treated with the same respect and reverence as her mother. She was in such a state of euphoria over winning that it perhaps did not dawn on her how her life had just changed forever. The Owens took their seats in the stands.

The ice dancers opened the program on Saturday. Ice dance today is famous for sometimes garish and gaudy costumes, judging collusion scandals, and beautiful, if somewhat strangely contortionist, moves. The sport did not start this way. In its beginnings ice dance was the same as any ballroom dance. Four different and distinct rhythms were expected in a well-balanced routine. Costumes resembled evening wear.

Today, ice dance is the least watched of the skating disciplines. One can surmise this is due to the lack of high-flying, dangerous tricks. Competitive skaters, though, know a truth most fans don't realize. Ice dancing takes a supreme ability to control muscles, sometimes moving the upper and lower bodies in opposite directions. The dance takes carriage, flow, and a complete mastery of every possible manipulation of the blade and its edges. Ice dance, for all the criticism it has received, is a true gift, and quite under appreciated.

In 1961, the real drama seemed to come before the event. Ice dance was not an Olympic event until the 1970s, so making it to the World Championships was the highest goal for any ice dance team.

Dallas "Larry" Pierce of Indianapolis was ready to give Worlds one last try. Larry and his partner, Marilyn Meeker, had been to Worlds once before, finishing fifth, but they had never won a medal. Larry wanted desperately to try to win a medal before retiring from competition.

With his lean face and thick-rimmed glasses, Larry resembled Buddy Holly, though he wore his hair in a buzz cut. Instead of the usual blue blood common in skating, Larry was more a blue-collar type. He liked collecting guns and taking photographs, served briefly in the Marines, and also attended Indiana University for two years. When he wasn't training, he helped his dad in the family plumbing

Photo courtesy of Richard Rosborough

Larry Pierce of Indianapolis and Diane Sherbloom of California began training together only five weeks before the 1961 U.S. National Championships.

business. Around the rink, he was known as a first-class comedian. Skating was hardly an activity you'd expect someone with Larry's background to be doing, but Sonja Henie had taken skating from the elite social clubs to corner movie theaters, bringing mass appeal to the sport. The burgeoning middle and upper-middle classes brought a new population of skating fans to the frozen ponds of America.

The sport was growing, but everyone knows the better you get at skating, the more expensive it becomes. The better you are, the more difficult your moves. Those moves cause the skates to wear out more quickly. Competitors performing double jumps in 1961 and practicing several hours a day could count on needing a new pair of skates every four to six months. A pair of skates in 1961 would cost between twenty-five dollars and one hundred dollars. Lessons, ice time, clothes, tights—it all added up to a sum most families simply could not afford. In 1961, there was no system of financial aid in place for skaters. It seemed the sport was destined to remain trapped in the sort of elitist realm that it had inhabited for so long.

Larry Pierce hardly fit into this mold. Indianapolis was only a minor center of skating, but he never allowed himself to feel like an outsider. His odds became even longer right before his last hurrah. Less than two months before the 1961 U.S. National Championships, Larry and Marilyn were running their routine, when she fell hard, sliding into the boards at the rink. She cringed in pain, and coaches Daniel and Rose Anne Ryan knew it was serious.

After a thorough examination, the doctor delivered some bad news. Marilyn had chipped a bone in her ankle and tore a ligament. She would need to be off the ice for at least two months. Skating at Nationals was out of the question.

Larry took the news hard, believing his last chance at world glory was gone. But then he started entertaining a crazy idea: "What if I could find another partner and get trained in time for Nationals?" Most ice dancers and pairs skaters spend years together, trying to find the rhythm that makes champions click, seeming to move as one on the ice. With Marilyn's blessing, however, Larry began his almost absurd quest to find a temporary replacement partner in time for Nationals.

Most female ice dancers who skated at Larry's level were paired with other skaters. But then, like a gift from heaven, he came across Diane Sherbloom. As a Pacific Coast Dance Champion, she was a proven competitor in the national ranks. Diane, also known as "Dee Dee," was a gorgeous, slender, eighteen-year-old blonde with blue eyes. She was a well-mannered, all-American girl.

The financial situation in the Sherbloom family, however, was not good for a figure skater. Dee Dee's father, a professional ice sculptor, was a paraplegic, due to injuries he sustained in an accident. The family didn't have the money to pay for her to travel to competitions, on top of coaching and ice time.

Larry, his parents, and his coach did everything they could to entice her to leave her Los Angeles home and travel to Indianapolis and train for the 1961 Nationals. They sent certified letters. They called numerous times. Larry's coaches, Daniel and Rose Anne, promised to put up Dee Dee for free in their home, already crowded with four children and another baby on the way. Larry's parents promised to care for Dee Dee as if she were their own daughter.

Dee Dee hesitated, feeling that even if she did win a medal at Nationals, it would really belong to Marilyn Meeker. And besides, her mother, little sister, and father needed her at home during that very trying time.

Larry begged, "Please, I have just one last shot."

The Sherbloom family ultimately left the decision to Dee Dee, and before she knew it, she was boarding a plane for Indianapolis. When she landed, this most unlikely pair had only five weeks to train before Nationals. Suddenly, they found themselves standing at the side of the rink, waiting for their turn to perform at the 1961 U.S. Nationals. They silently watched the favorites take the ice.

Larry and Dee Dee viewed one pair as a particular threat for gold. Eighteen-year-old Roger Campbell and twenty-year-old Dona Lee Carrier from Los Angeles were skating in their first Nationals together. They had a polished, flashy look about them on the ice. They both attended the Hollywood Professional School, which was famous for educating child stars, and in some cases, famous young athletes. Each had enjoyed some success competing with other partners but decided to team up when prior partnerships ended.

Dona Lee was the daughter of a minister. He had moved the family from New York to Los Angeles when she was a teenager. Skating made the move seem like less of a change. As with many skaters, training served as the great constant in her life.

Their skating exuded a silky quality, and their presentation was as elegant as a posh black-tie affair. Their routine went from a waltz to a jazz beat, and they handled both styles expertly. Because they skated first, it seemed the judges weren't ready to hand out high scores, even when deserved.

Larry and Dee Dee knew they were next.

The announcer intoned, "He represents the Winter Club of Indianapolis, and she represents the Los Angeles Figure Skating Club. Please welcome Larry Pierce and Diane Sherbloom."

Larry bit his lower lip as he put his hand on Dee Dee's waist to start their performance. Larry and Diane were very much a study in physical contrast on the ice. At 5'2", Diane was a full eight inches shorter than Larry. Most coaches would never have paired them had desperate circumstances not prevailed.

During the first half of their routine, Larry nearly tripped and fell but somehow kept his cool and maintained his speed. Even with that mistake and the lack of preparation, Larry and Dee Dee earned high marks, and they took the lead. There was only one pair left that could spoil their hopes for victory.

This final team also raced the clock in preparation for Nationals. New York newlyweds Robert and Patricia Dineen were a rarity in competitive skating: They were new parents. Bob and Pat had never before skated in the top level at Nationals. Just as they started winning important tournaments, news of Pat's delicate condition put their competitive careers on hold. Just seven months before Nationals, Pat gave birth to a healthy baby boy, Robert, Jr.

This was Ron Ludington's first really successful turn as a coach. Full-time coaching jobs were a competitive business due to the small number of year-round rinks. In those days, coaches were simply called "pros." Ron aspired to be a full-time pro somewhere, anywhere, but the jobs just weren't available. As he coached the

Dineens, he was living lean in a Connecticut YMCA, commuting to New York for the lessons. Ron and his wife, Olympic bronze medalist Nancy Ludington, were in the midst of a divorce. Adding to the stress was the uncertainty that he could get Bob and Pat ready for the Nationals event.

Bob worked for the Pension and Welfare Fund in New York but planned to go to law school. Pat was a statistical clerk for the Sterling Drug Company. They both loved swimming, water skiing, and music. Bob collected records, and Pat played the piano. All other interests would have to stop while they trained in every spare moment for their big shot at a trip to Prague. When the time came for Nationals, Pat was barely ready. On the off chance that they would make the world team and need to go to Prague, they had made arrangements with Bob's brother to keep the baby while they were away.

Bob and Pat knew they had nothing to lose. It is in precisely these moments that some skaters perform beyond their capabilities. Sarah Hughes is a great modern example. She had never won a major national or international championship. She was considered a long shot for a medal in the 2002 Winter Olympic Games. All eyes were on Michelle Kwan, who was expected to win and retire from the sport. Sarah and her coach shared the same philosophy—"Let it all go. There's nothing to lose here." Had the Russian-Canadian judging scandal not erupted, there is a very strong chance the judges would have given the gold medal to Russian Irina Slutskaya, a terrific skater who made one small mistake in her program. Sarah, however, was perfect. She rose to the occasion in one of the most memorable skating performances of the decade. The judges, under the world's microscope, had no choice but to give the gold to the true winner.

Bob and Pat had no real expectations. Yet they performed a clean program. There were no sudden lapses in concentration, no falls, no hiccups.

The ice dance podium looked like this:

Gold: Larry Pierce and Diane Sherbloom
Silver: Roger Campbell and Dona Lee Carrier
Bronze: Robert and Patricia Dineen

The men were last on the itinerary. The event seemed destined to belong to Tim Brown, who at one point placed third in the world. He was studying to be a zoologist and appeared to be cutting back on his training. Surprisingly, he was ranked third after the school figures. As he took the ice for the free skate, pain shot through his chest. He had trouble landing any of his jumps, putting his second foot down on most of them. He would be very lucky to hold on to a medal at all, much less make the world team. He planned to see a doctor about his chest tightness as soon as he could.

Douglas Ramsay, representing the Skating Club of Detroit, was next to skate. The sixteen-year-old looked to be more a child of thirteen than a young man of sixteen. He had become famous for barely squeaking out a victory against Maribel's student Frank Carroll in the junior division of the U.S Championships the year before. Maribel was stunned by this child, who seemed to come out of nowhere.

Every now and then, a skater bursts onto the scene and one thinks, "That kid is going to be a star." Doug was that skater in 1961. The audience thought he was a darling.

He charmed them with amazing showmanship and managed to land a triple jump, making him the only man in the field to even try one. Surprisingly, he finished behind Tim Brown, because he hadn't done well in the school figures. It seemed his chances at a trip to Prague were gone, even though he seemed to have the greatest raw talent of the field.

Gregory Kelley was next. He was the leader after the school figures and was favored to win. The Kelley family had made tremendous sacrifices to keep Gregory in skates. His twenty-eight-year-old sister, Nathalie, a science teacher in Boston, took a sabbatical at her parents' urging when Gregory decided to move from the Boston Skating Club to Colorado Springs to train with Edi Scholdan. She went to Colorado to be Gregory's chaperone. The Broadmoor Figure Skating Club welcomed them with open arms, in the same way they had welcomed the Westerfeld girls.

Gregory and Nathalie were the children of Dr. and Mrs. Vincent Kelley of Newton Centre, Massachusetts, who had six other children. Gregory wanted to be a doctor like his father but first wanted to live up to his potential in skating. Gregory also enjoyed water skiing, but he had his academic side, too. He was a member of the American Numismatic Association and was credited with having the world's largest collection of three-dollar bills. Only sixty-five were known to exist, and Kelley somehow collected forty-two of them.

Gregory considered himself his biggest competitor, as he explained quite eloquently to reporters leading up to Nationals. "When I am on the ice, I'm not trying to compete against the other skaters," he said. "Instead, I'm thinking of my own ability and trying to top it with the finest performance of which I am capable."

Coach Edi Scholdan thought Gregory was capable of someday winning an Olympic gold medal, because he possessed the perfect blend of athletic and artistic ability. His artistic flair, however, sometimes got him into trouble. Once, he dyed a portion of his jet-black hair to a bright blonde color. He was advised that the color would have to go, or the judges would penalize him for it.

He won the U.S. junior men's title in 1959, moved up to the senior level the next year, and was named second alternate to the world team. As a team alternate, he was called on short notice to skate at the World Championships in 1960, when the Olympians decided to retire. He placed a respectable ninth. Edi Scholdan was confident that with more preparation time, Kelley could place in the top three at the World Championships in Prague. Nathalie planned to accompany him.

At Nationals, Gregory lived up to his reputation in a nearly flawless free skate. Oddsmakers would have placed money on him to win, but there was a spoiler in the wings. Bradley Lord, the reserved and serious twenty-one-year-old, had taken a leave of absence from his senior year at Boston College in order to train. He had missed making the 1960 Olympic team by 94/100ths of a point. He, like Kelley, was called to compete at the 1960 World Championships, where he placed sixth.

In second place after the compulsory figures, Bradley needed to be perfect to win. Tackling the elements one at a time, he executed each jump to perfection. With scores ranging from 5.5 to 5.8, Lord won the title.

The men's world team was:

Gold: Bradley Lord

Silver: Gregory Kelley

Bronze: Tim Brown

Winning skaters were presented with medals and trophies. In the dance and pairs event, each team member would keep the trophy for half the year before returning it to the U.S. Figure Skating Association for the next American championship. The champions posed with their new hardware. Other competitors felt they had suffered the most profound heartbreak of their lives.

After the event, all the skaters were treated to the customary celebration dance. They danced until two in the morning, with that special vitality that rushes through the veins of the young. If they were lucky, they would be allowed to sleep late the next morning.

The greatest victories of all belonged perhaps to Maribel. Her daughters were now American champions, just like she was. Laurence especially seemed on pace to claim the Olympic glory

Courtesy of the Winchester Massachusetts Archival Center

Laurence Owen, Maribel Vinson Owen, and Maribel Y. Owen display their growing trophy collection to a photographer.

denied Maribel in her prime. Then there was Myra Westerfeld. At the most pivotal moment in Steffi's life, she was abandoned by her husband and forced to live on the charity of others. She had endured a dramatic and sudden lifestyle change. While the medal draped around Steffi's neck was not the gold they had all wanted, it was still a medal at Nationals, something never before achieved in this skating family. Most significant for her, perhaps, was that Otto could not take credit for the accomplishment. He stopped participating in the skating lifestyle as Steffi made her breakthrough. Myra, through her devotion, and Sherri, through her self-sacrifice, had made this happen, and Otto would be shut out of the victory celebration. If the celebration was somewhat bittersweet, it nonetheless held a good bit of satisfaction for all the Westerfeld women.

Laurence was the new "queen of the ice." Steffi would have to settle for the role of princess for now. But both regal titles were cause for great celebration.

All celebrating, however, would be cut short. The North American Championships were just two weeks away, and there was no time to waste.

Chapter Seven

"Praha, 22-26 Unora, 1961."

Laurence beamed with pride as she held the tiny pin in her hands. The words were written in Czech. In English, the trinket would have read, "Prague, 22-26, February, 1961." The traces of rainbow-colored skate blades danced across the gold plating.

In addition to medals and trophies, each member of the newly selected World Championships team was given a special commemorative pin. One is minted for each major skating championship, and the pins inspire a collecting craze among die-hard skating fans. Coaches and event organizers at the 1961 Nationals had been given these tokens, too, along with their counterparts in Prague, who were readying their city's venue for the World Championships. The pins would be made available for sale to the public only at the commencement in Prague.

"I think this is my new good luck charm," Laurence may have said, tucking her chin to properly fasten it to her favorite practice sweater. "There. Perfect."

It would be cumbersome to wear the championships medals to skating practice, but the little pin would surely stay in place. Many

The 1961 Prague World Championships pin.

Photo courtesy of the Broadmoor Hotel

fellow Boston skaters had the same pin.

With the North American Championships briskly approaching, the Owen family was back to its usual time-strapped ways—practice, school, and more practice. February 11 and 12 marked the dates the North Americans were to take place in Philadelphia.

Fortunately, there was a morsel of time to revel in the victories that had taken place just a few days earlier. The *CBS Sports Spectacular* was going to be on television. The atmosphere was electric in the Owen and Westerfeld homes as well as in the homes of all the athletes who had competed at Nationals.

Skaters in 1961 didn't have the luxury to see themselves perform very often. For the 1961 Worlds team, this television broadcast likely would have been a first. Today, video cameras are a staple at many practice sessions. The playback feature is such a vital tool in any critique session. From a video, the skater and coach can carefully dissect each portion of the jump—takeoff, rotation, and landing—and discern what needs the most work.

Granny Owen, too frail to travel to Colorado Springs to see the event live, was finally able to see what her granddaughters had accomplished. She gingerly took her place on the tan upholstered couch so rarely used amid the constant comings and goings of the Owen home.

In Colorado Springs, the Westerfelds prepared Steffi's favorite snack before the show began. The smell of popcorn wafted through their apartment. Myra made hasty reminder calls to family members across the country about the broadcast, and shared the news of Steffi's impending stardom to all who would listen. The commotion caused Seric to occasionally let out a high-pitched yelp befitting a small dog, but Steffi scooped him up and drew him close to her, and he reciprocated by licking her face.

"Hurry and turn on your sets," Myra said to neighbors and anyone who called on the telephone. In the back of her mind, Steffi must have wondered if her father was watching in Kansas City.

As the show introduction rolled, each of the skater's households erupted into a chorus of "Shhhhhh! It's on now!"

The broadcast began with a short, on-camera introduction sans dramatic writing or music. Host Bud Palmer, a common sight in televised sports events of the era, welcomed the television audience to the U.S National Figure Skating Championship. Two-time Olympic skating gold medalist Dick Button stood beside him and provided color commentary. Next to Big Maribel, Button was perhaps the leading American authority on skating. He had been the first skater ever to land a triple jump in competition, pushing the technical limits of the sport in a time when a triple jump was thought impossible. Button, who is now a staple at any major amateur skating event in the U.S., was getting his first real sample of life on television, although in those days, he had not yet developed his now-famous fixation on spin positions.

There were no pre-packaged stories during which the public

would learn about the many sacrifices of training, the agonizing losses, or the personal lives of the competitors. There was no "kiss and cry" area, where breathless skaters waited with their coaches for the results. There were no computer-generated graphics that showed the scores. When scores were announced, the camera simply focused on the old-fashioned scorecards each judge held up.

One of the most entertaining portions of the broadcast, at least to our eyes today, was the commercials. The first commercial was for L&M cigarettes, a key sponsor. Perhaps created specifically to run with the event, the commercial featured two professional pairs skaters, moving across the ice while a commentator described their maneuvers. After some lovely lifts and footwork, the skaters glided to the boards, where the commentator met them, and said, "Sure looks like you could use an L&M cigarette." The skaters then began smoking and talking about the "delicious tobacco taste."

The commentator urged them to continue skating now that they were properly "recharged," and they skated off—cigarettes hanging from their mouths. The rest of the commercials were divided between Schlitz beer and cars. Back then, network demographic researchers and television sales executives had not yet determined that the primary audience of figure skating is women.

The CBS television producers made some interesting choices in what was shown and what was omitted during the hour. In the pairs event, rather than show the performances of the three medalists, they elected to cut Laurie and Bill Hickox, the bronze medalists, in favor of the junior champions, Ronald and Vivian Joseph. Laurie's and Bill's parents, watching from San Francisco, very likely had a strong word or two for the broadcast's editors. It is uncertain if Bill, living in the barracks of the Air Force Academy, would have had access to a television to watch his triumph even if it had been shown.

In the dance event, only the top two teams were shown, and Dick Button opined that Dona Lee Carrier and Roger Campbell were one of the best teams he had ever seen. At the very least, this team should have won Nationals that year over the less polished Larry Pierce and Diane Sherbloom. The judges disagreed and placed them in the silver-medal position.

The marquee ladies event, just as it was during the championship, was not saved for last as it is today. It was shown second. The top three finishers were shown. Dick marveled at Rhode's speed. Known for being somewhat harsh on competitors today, he was perhaps too kind to Steffi, downplaying her missed jumps, and instead remarking on her refined appearance and presentation. During Laurence's performance, the commentating remained similarly low key, the two commentators apparently less enchanted by Laurence than the audience. They instead focused on her Olympic and World team experience.

In today's over-hyped, emotion-packed sports broadcasts, the history being made at the 1961 Nationals would likely be the subject of mass promotion and intense discussion. The fact that Laurence and Mara were chasing their mother's old titles was barely acknowledged. Only one other skating family could boast similar success—the Jenkins brothers, Hayes Alan and David, who won Olympic gold medals in 1956 and 1960, respectively. Fellow 1960 gold medalist Carol Heiss married Hayes Alan Jenkins in 1960, creating another powerhouse skating family.

Perhaps a testament to the great gender divide at the time, the broadcast gave more airtime to the men's singles competition than any other event. Doug Ramsay, who had been given the nickname "Dick Button, Junior," was the only fourth-place skater shown from the singles events.

After each event, the gold medalists appeared on camera for an interview with Bud Palmer. Mara and Dud did the first interview. Mara seemed visibly nervous and fidgety on camera, letting Dudley take the lead. He took charge and seemed to be a natural, confidently asserting his eagerness "to get back to the real estate business." Bud commented on how in the Owen household, there must not be room for many more trophies. Mara tepidly whispered, "No, not really."

Laurence was interviewed next, and if her skating was not cause for the audience to fall in love with her, certainly her unbridled enthusiasm must have won over the viewers. Laurence's giddiness shone through as she exclaimed, "Golly, I feel terrific," in response to the question of how the victory felt. She smiled the entire time she talked, her unsure eyes shifting between the camera and the interviewer. She didn't have any kind of pretentiousness about her; she seemed just like a regular young girl still unaccustomed to all the attention she was receiving. Her arms seemed heavy at her sides as she fought to keep her grip on the tall champion's trophy.

Bud Palmer interviewed the champions of the dance event following their skate. Larry Pierce gave all the credit to his coach. "We figure Dan Ryan is one of the best pros in the country," he said. "We're gonna go back to Indianapolis and train there, then go to North Americans, then go to Prague." During the interview, something struck Larry as funny, and he scooted out of the camera's view to conceal his laughter. Dee Dee maintained her composure as it was pointed out that she was not Larry's "regular" partner.

When the men's scores were announced, Dick Button viewed the men's result as somewhat of an upset. In an interview following the event, Bradley Lord exhibited modesty uncharacteristic of many of today's athletes, when he mentioned how certain he was of Gregory Kelley's victory. Lord just smiled and said, "I sort of thought he would [win] too. After I skated, I thought I did the best I could."

Modest, attractive, standout American youngsters they all seemed to be. Now the American public began to fall in love with them. Laurence received fan mail by the ten-pound bag. Little girls already looked up to her, writing her sweet letters, such as, "Dear Laurence, you are a pretty skater. I liked your dress."

Photo courtesy of Richard Rosborough

Former world ice dance bronze medalist Daniel Ryan and wife Rose Anne trained skaters, including Larry Pierce and Diane Sherbloom, at the Winter Club of Indianapolis.

Steffi received similar letters. She also seemed to attract a fair amount of interest from older men, much to the consternation of her mother. Myra became especially worried when one man started sending flowers to Steffi every day at the rink. She called the flower shop to have delivery stopped.

Myra was right to worry, though in those more innocent times, security wasn't much of a consideration for the athletes. In figure skating, little thought was given to it at all, at least until the famous Nancy Kerrigan attack. Now, if you want to gain access to a practice session at the Broadmoor World Arena, you must sign in with a front office clerk. Unfortunately, not all rinks take the public threat seriously. Many world-class training facilities lack security. Even at major events, security lapses can be a threat to the athletes. Michelle Kwan, as she prepared for her free skate at the 2004 World Championships in Dortmund, Germany, was followed onto the ice by a tutu-clad man with a casino advertisement painted on his bare chest. The man was arrested, and Michelle Kwan managed to shake off the incident on her way to a bronze-medal finish.

Despite any perceived danger, Steffi and Laurence were greatly flattered by the fan letters, though there was hardly time to read them, much less respond to each well-wisher. The next six weeks would be the busiest of the skaters' lives.

After Nationals, the competitors shifted their focus to the North American Championships, the most competitive event in which American skaters could compete next to the World Championships and the Olympics. Winning a medal at the North Americans was vitally important, because losing there would almost assure a loss at Worlds. The Americans had some tough competition. Laurence, Steffi, and Rhode would see their biggest challenge from Canadian champion Wendy Griner. Laurence and Wendy had competed against each other twice in 1960—at the Olympics and Worlds. Laurence placed sixth to Wendy's twelfth at the Olympics, and ninth to Wendy's seventh at Worlds. In the pairs event, the Canadian siblings Otto and Maria Jelinek were the biggest competition for Mara and Dud. They had won a silver medal at Worlds the year before and were fourth at the Olympics. They also had two Worlds bronze medals in their collection. Mara and Dud were considered definite underdogs.

In the men's event, Donald Jackson, the reigning Olympic bronze medalist and World silver medalist, was the clear favorite. Canadians Virginia Thompson and William McLachlan were heavily favored in the dance event, after a silver medal finish at the

1960 Worlds, the same event at which Larry Pierce and his partner Marilyn Meeker had placed fifth.

The competition came only every other year, and this time around, it presented a unique dilemma. The flight to Prague departed only two days after the North Americans. It didn't seem to make any sense for the skaters to go back to their home cities for such a short amount of time. United States Figure Skating Association leaders had decided it would make more sense for the team to travel by bus for two hours from Philadelphia to New York, and fly together to Prague, where they would have a few days to adjust their body clocks to the time difference (for the Californians, that was ten hours), then spend a few days practicing for the event.

Making the flight arrangements was in itself quite difficult. International flights were less commonplace than they are in today's era of modern business travel, and the Cold War created anxiety among some of the skaters, many of whom had never flown overseas before. Contributing to the fears was that on March 29, 1960, a Soviet-made Ilyushin turboprop plane operating for Czechoslovak Air crashed north of Nuremberg, Germany, killing all on board. Some of the athletes and their families wanted assurances that no Russian parts were used in their plane. Some expressed a fear of sabotage.

There were no direct flights to Prague available in February of 1961. Each flight option included a stop in Brussels, Belgium, for refueling. Sabena was the only airline that offered flights to Brussels on American-made Boeing 707s, and that operated American-made Douglas aircraft on the second leg of the trip to Prague. Pan American Airlines and Trans World Airlines offered service on American-made aircraft only to Brussels. Czechoslovak Air, which used Russian-made planes, was the only other available airline offering flights from Brussels to Prague. Sabena, taking into consideration all the concerns of the U.S. skating delegation, was the obvious choice. Its international travel office even offered assistance to U.S. skaters who needed help obtaining travel visas. In addition, Sabena assured the USFSA that should the Brussels-bound flight arrive late, the Prague-bound flight would wait for them before taking off.

Following Worlds, the skaters had been booked to skate exhibitions in front of European audiences. Even some of the junior skaters were invited to participate. The nearly three weeks away from home would be the longest some of them had been away from their parents. The tickets cost $602, half the price of a new Volkswagen Beetle. For this reason, most of the parents knew they would not be able to afford the trip.

The Westerfelds did manage to collect enough money for one ticket. Myra felt it would be beneficial for Sherri to go. Myra had been battling high blood pressure and had not been feeling well, anyway. Additionally, Myra often made Steffi more nervous with her constant critiques, while Sherri helped ease Steffi's nerves. Besides, Sherri deserved to go. She had spent so much of her own money helping Steffi attain her dreams, that this would be a welcome reward for all the sacrifice. Sherri was thrilled to be going to Europe, particularly with her sister. The divorce, Myra's moods, and the commonality of understanding the sport had made them closer than ever. They looked forward to experiencing Europe together.

In 1961, the United States Figure Skating Association paid the bare minimum to skaters traveling abroad. Plane tickets and hotels for skaters and the American judges were covered, but meals were not. Coaches received no reimbursement of expenses whatsoever. Despite the heavy financial burden, coaches felt it necessary to accompany their athletes to such a significant event. Steffi's coach, Edi Scholdan, had decided to bring his son, James, and planned to return to his native Austria after the other team members had gone home.

Only two coaches were unable to make the trip: Ron Ludington and Montgomery "Bud Wilson." Wilson was Bradley Lord's coach, and was needed in Boston to help plan the club's big annual show, called "Ice Chips." Ron Ludington had some good news and bad news for his team, Robert and Patricia Dineen. The bad news was that he could not secure the cash to make the trip. The good news was that his close friend Daniel Ryan would act as their interim coach while abroad. The disappointed Dineens asked, "Are you sure you can't go?" But Ron had pinched every penny to no avail. The trip was off.

Some clubs resorted to fundraisers to make sure coaches could go. In Washington State, the Seattle Skating Club threw a good-bye party for the U.S. pairs silver medalists, Ila Ray and Ray Hadley, and their stepmother and coach, Alvah Hadley. As a good-luck charm, the club gave Ila Ray and Ray a silver dollar each, so they wouldn't forget their club back home.

Money was not the only potential hindrance for the skaters and coaches. It appeared for a time that Air Cadet William Hickox and his sister Laurie would not be able to make the trip, despite their bronze medal in the pairs event at Nationals. Bill was awaiting special permission from the Air Force to travel overseas. At the eleventh hour, they were still waiting, and becoming less hopeful and more emotionally stressed by the hour. Vivian and Ronald Joseph, the pairs alternates, were throwing clothes into suitcases and rushing to prepare themselves to go to Europe, too.

Tim Brown, the American men's bronze medalist, was still having trouble with chest pains and shortness of breath. He consulted with a doctor, who didn't have good news. The diagnosis was rheumatic fever, a painful condition that causes inflammation in the joints and in serious cases, the heart valves. Tim was ordered to stop skating immediately. He contacted the USFSA to tell them he could not go to either North Americans or Prague. Tim never skated competitively again.

Douglas Ramsay was named first alternate to the World team but was not expecting to go. One evening, the phone rang in his Detroit home. The USFSA informed Doug that he was needed to fill in at North Americans and Worlds.

"Yes!" he screeched.

Doug was ready to take on the world. He felt like the luckiest boy alive. He wasn't expecting this fortunate turn of events but planned to capitalize by working extra hard on his school figures the next morning in practice. He would also need to quickly pack. Doug had never traveled overseas before, but he had good advice when it came to packing.

With the overseas flight came many restrictions on baggage. Each passenger was allowed only forty-four pounds in baggage weight. Squaw Valley Olympic gold medalists Carol Heiss and David Jenkins wrote letters to the skaters, advising them how to pack.

In Carol's letter, she counseled the ladies: "I always bring two skating dresses for practice and for the compulsory figures I wear a dress. Bring an extra pair of tights as they do not sell the American Danskins in Europe. Be sure to bring nylon stockings, Kleenex tissues (as they are expensive in Europe), and your favorite cosmetics. Remember—for your entire trip never let go of your skates and records because they are the most important items! Good luck to all for a wonderful and successful trip to Europe!"

David Jenkins advised the young men making the trip: "A certain amount of sacrifice is entailed in the choosing of the wardrobe for the trip to the Championship abroad. My first sacrifice is the tux. There has been in the past just one possible occasion to use the tux, the banquet after the Championships! The officials usually wear the tux, but few others do. In its place I have previously taken one dark suit, which is adequate for this banquet and all the other numerous occasions which require dress-up attire. Loads of luck to everyone—it's an experience you will never forget."

Maribel Vinson Owen was especially busy, as she readied herself and her two daughters for the trip.

She sent a letter to U.S. skating administrator H. Kendall Kelley:

> Dear Ken,
>
> Herewith enclosed two grisly pictures for my visa application, which Maribel Jr. made for me yesterday morning, also a check for the seventeen-day excursion made out as Dudley directed. It would help our training (also our packing) if we knew the exact conditions of the rink—size, outdoor or roofed over, etc. Do you suppose you could reply to these points within a few days? I understand Prague has a wonderful hotel these days, the Yalta, and many fine restaurants—a far cry from my last visit there in 1934!
>
> See you in Philadelphia—Colorado Springs was exciting—We're holding the thumbs for the North Americans—the next step.
>
> As ever—in great haste,
>
> Maribel Sr.

Between last-minute packing and practice, Maribel and her daughters were getting their pictures taken for an article in the *Boston Herald*. During the photo shoot, the reporter reminded Maribel of her outburst against European judges just a year earlier in Squaw Valley.

"Let's talk about that later," she said curtly. "Let's hope those judges in Prague are back on the beam as to careful judging in the compulsory school figures. I'll give you a call when we get back from Europe and tell you about it."

Joy erupted in Colorado Springs when the Air Force came through for Laurie and Bill Hickox. Bill was granted a special military order excusing him from his duties so he could pursue a world championship.

The last week of February 1961 was filled with festive good-bye parties, the doling out of good luck charms, and the long embraces of those feeling the crushing pangs of parenthood as they let a child go on a fantastic journey.

Sixteen-year-old Douglas Ramsay's mother was supposed to go with him, but her duties to her other children intervened. Jean Ramsay was needed at home in Detroit, Michigan, to care for another child who had severe asthma. She was slightly comforted by the fact that Doug's coach, Bill Swallender, was still going to Europe. Before Doug left for Philadelphia, Mrs. Ramsay gave her son a handful of silver dollars for luck.

Diana LeMaire hugged her father, Edward, in the driveway of their Rye, New York, home. Edward was scheduled to go to Worlds to observe because he was to judge the following year. His specific marching orders included developing ways to understand and fight the pressure applied by Eastern-bloc judges. He decided to take his thirteen-year-old son, Richard, with him. "Dickie" had missed an entire term of school after a bout with osteomyelitis, and his father thought seeing distant lands would prove more educational than sitting in what Dickie viewed as the most supreme form of torture—eighth grade.

As they loaded the car and prepared to drive into the city and off to Idlewild Airport, Dickie gave his little sister a noogie, accompanied by, "See ya, squirt!"

Indianapolis coach Daniel Ryan and his wife, Rose Anne, had guided the national ice dance champions to victory together in 1961, but they would not travel to the World Championships together. Rose Anne would stay behind in Indianapolis caring for the couple's five children. A baby boy was born just two weeks before North Americans. Before leaving his house in Indianapolis, he knelt down to his six-year-old son, Kevin, and said, "I am going to be gone for a long time. You are the man of the house, so take good care of your mother."

Granny Vinson watched her daughter and granddaughters heave their suitcases down the stairs. She did not shed a tear, but pecked each on the cheek. She had lived in the sprawling house alone before, but remarked that it would be eerily quiet once they left.

Myra sobbed at the airport. She embraced her daughters tightly, promising each hug or kiss would be the last, only to break that promise a few tearful moments later. She had never let the girls out of her sight for any substantial amount of time, and this trip would surely test her frayed nerves. Myra was ill at ease about her daughters going on the plane, but Sherri's assuring voice helped calm her.

Edi Scholdan was preparing to fly from Denver to Philadelphia for the North American Championships with his three pupils and their family members. Edi disliked flying, though he had done it many times. A *Denver Post* reporter, Lee Meade, was supposed to accompany Scholdan on the trip, but at the last moment, his boss said, "You're not going to report on the World Championships. Next year." Lee went to the airport to wish everyone luck. He knew Scholdan was afraid of flying, and played to that fear. Lee noticed some black smoke rising from a trash fire near the airport. He looked at Scholdan and said, "Edi, that's your plane now, it's burning." To this, Scholdan replied without looking, "Well, that's all right. Whenever someone can tell me if my plane is burning or when I can read about it in the newspapers, I will not be worried about it. If the day comes that my plane crashed and I do not hear of it, then I'll be very upset."

Chapter Eight

The bone-buckling February frost clung to the windows of the Philadelphia Figure Skating Club and Humane Society.

"Humane Society?" skaters would ask quizzically as they read the signs on the rink doors, before they burst into laughter.

The arena name had nothing at all to do with the rescue of animals as one would expect. Rather, this humane society endeavored to rescue people. Its ties to the skating rink came almost a century earlier, when the club was first formed as a gentlemen's athletic club, which also served to rescue poor souls who crashed into icy Pennsylvania ponds while skating. The club members even carried badges that made them a sort of civilian police entity.

The Philadelphia Skating Club and Humane Society was the first figure skating club in the United States and was host to the first-ever U.S. Championships, giving it the storied past that qualified it for "sacred ground" status. Once the indoor rink was built, the "humane society" portion of the name stuck.

Whatever the origins of its name, the lobby's warmth could not come fast enough for the weary travelers, who just the night before had landed on a snow-dusted tarmac before driving to the hotel

AP Images

Four champions enjoy their newfound celebrity at the 1961 North American Championships. From left: U.S. men's champion Bradley Lord, U.S. ladies champion Laurence Owen, Canadian ladies champion Wendy Griner, and Canadian men's champion Don Jackson.

they would call home for five days. Wakeup calls for three, four, or five in the morning were not the usual for guests, but these guests were tenacious in their quest for victory—they were the figure skating elite from two countries.

The Americans and Canadians all arrived at the heavily arched rink building, their earmuffs and gloves bundling their extremities in a fierce fight against the cold. Inside, the frigid air would be exacerbated by wind created by skating fast, a gust that felt more like a jet stream against their chafed faces. Mara and Dud made their way to the practice ice rink, holding hands as usual.

A lone ice monitor ushered the first of the groggy, sleepy-eyed skaters to the rink door, with coffee-slurping coaches tailing behind. Their names were called in militaristic fashion.

"Maria and Otto Jelinek."

"Here."

"Dudley Richards and Maribel Y. Owen."

"Here."

"Gertrude Desjardins and Maurice Lafrance."

"Present."

Names continued to ring out. Most of these teams had never competed against each other before. However, Maria and Otto Jelinek, a sister-and-brother team favored to win the gold, had met Mara Owen and Dudley Richards while skating exhibitions in America. The two teams greeted each other with the same sincere handshakes, hugs, and pecks on the cheek that one would expect from friends returning to summer camp. The North American Championships to them were almost not a competition, but more of a class reunion in this closely knit world.

Maria and Otto originally hailed from Czechoslovakia. Their parents had defected from the communist regime years earlier so Maria and Otto could live a life of freedom. When the Jelineks won their Canadian national title in 1961, they earned passage to the World Championships in Prague. The Czech government threatened to have them arrested if they entered the country. The International Skating Union, in turn, threatened to remove the event from Prague if the Jelineks were harassed in any way. A reluctant truce had been brokered on their behalf, but the Jelineks confided in Mara and Dud their fear of returning to their homeland.

A plan was hatched. The Jelineks and Mara and Dud came to an agreement that the safest way to be ignored by the Czechs was to arrive on the American team plane. The Canadian and American planes were departing at roughly the same time. It was decided the Jelineks would meet the Americans at Idlewild Airport on departure day and organize a switch with someone so they could fly with the Americans. This way, the Jelineks would be much less noticeable when they returned to Prague, and they'd feel safer.

The camaraderie extended beyond the pairs event. Laurence Owen and Canadian Wendy Griner were the reigning ice queens of the event. They were both the darlings of the sport, and their admiration for each other was natural. Laurence, Wendy, U.S. men's champion Bradley Lord, and Canadian men's champion Don Jackson spent time discussing their triumphs and, when spotting them together, photographers snapped as many pictures as they could. The young skaters basked in the attention, smiling and posing, and carrying on as if there wasn't a competition at all. Laurence's one-of-a-kind smile eclipsed all others in photographs—every eye being drawn to her first by her uncanny magnetism. The carefree media blitz did not last long.

Each competitor or pairs team was allowed to run their programs, without any other skaters on the ice. Dud and Mara drew an early run-through time, and instead of skating their program cleanly, they stopped midway through and collapsed to the ice in fits of laughter over something Dudley said. Maribel stood watch and demanded to know what was so funny that they couldn't finish their routine, but they were laughing so hard they couldn't answer her. Maribel, Laurence, Dud, and Mara left the rink in search of food and rest for the competition. The competition got underway the next day, and they needed to retire early.

Maria and Otto started to run their routine. Not far into the program, disaster struck. Otto tripped while lifting Maria into a simple ballet position, and they became tangled with each other on the way down. Otto hit his head—something every skater fears. Every skater is taught in the beginning how to properly fall. Just as race car drivers lift their hands from the steering wheel before hitting the wall, skaters lift their hands to prevent breaking any bones when crashing to the ice. The maneuver becomes almost automatic after hundreds of falls. All efforts are made to keep the head away from the ice. Sometimes, things just happen too fast, even for world-class competitors like Otto and Maria. When it comes to the really nasty, body-bruising falls, everyone's number comes up once in a while. This time, Otto was knocked unconscious. His skate had gashed Maria's leg, and blood spilled onto the ice. The skaters at the rink, mostly Canadians by that time, poured onto the ice, along with Maria and Otto's coach, Bruce Hyland, to assess the situation. Maria was crying and gasping. Otto was knocked out. The two were rushed to the nearest hospital. It appeared that less than twenty-four hours before the North American pairs title would be decided, the front-runners were out of the competition.

At the hotel, the other Canadian skaters informed the Americans. Mara and Dud were stunned and wanted to go to the hospital. Maribel wouldn't hear of it. Even though this increased the odds of Dud and Mara winning, their concern for their dear friends overwhelmed them. Sleep would surely be difficult this night. Mara lingered outside the wide-open hotel room where Laurence and Maribel discussed the next day's schedule. As Dud turned the key to open his room, the two met between the doors and embraced.

"They'll be fine," Dud likely assured Mara. "Get some sleep and don't let it upset you." He pecked her on the forehead and she mustered a smile. Mara was a worrier, but in this case, there really was nothing she could do.

Everyone was anxious for news from the hospital. Most were certain the Jelineks would have to withdraw from the event. If they did withdraw, they would not be the first casualties of this competition. Rhode Michelson, the famously fast, "speed at all costs" skater, had taken her mantra to spectacular new levels in her program run-through the day before Maria and Otto's accident. Performing a double Salchow jump, her least secure jump, she didn't go "straight up," tilting, instead, in the air. Once a skater develops a lean in the air, it's very difficult to regain balance for a clean landing. Rhode simply could not recover from the mistake. At U.S. Nationals, she was so relieved to nail the jump, she clapped her hands together in celebration. This time, she was not so lucky. Perhaps she rushed the takeoff. Perhaps the increased speed could not be controlled. Whatever the cause, the fall that followed was the kind everyone at the rink hears. And every skater knows that if you can hear the impact, it's probably serious. Rhode landed on her right hip, which was her landing leg. One of the great questions skaters ponder is, "If you had to injure one leg over the other, which would it be—the landing leg, or the 'free' leg?" It's really tantamount to asking someone if they'd rather be deaf or blind. Both choices are catastrophic. Rhode could hear her hipbone pop out of its joint. Most skaters have a high tolerance for pain. When a fall actually brings tears, that generally means trouble.

Rhode managed to stand on the ice, but she quite noticeably favored the other leg as she grimaced in pain and skated gingerly to the boards. Her coach, William Kipp, was there to assist her to a bench. Without even speaking, they both knew to remove her skates. As each skate was pulled off, her face tightened to conceal the groans. The rink trainer was summoned to look at Rhode's hip. The recommendation was an ice pack—and no skating for at least three days. Rhode, in tears, informed the referee of her withdrawal from the North American Championships. She wasn't even sure she'd be able to skate at the World Championships. The United States Figure Skating Association was informed, and they made lightning-fast arrangements to fly U.S. ladies first alternate Karen Howland from Idaho to Philadelphia. She was asked to pack enough for the World Championships, too. Doctors would assess the situation again on February 13, giving Rhode just three days to recover in time to pursue her dream. She called home and shared the news with her parents, who both stretched the family income as far as it could go to keep Rhode and her brother in skates. How comforting the presence of her mother would have been, but the shared grief would have to take place through a static-filled phone line connecting Philadelphia to California.

The morning clocks stirred the skaters into a frenetic dance of showering and moving swiftly to the rink. Almost everyone woke up wondering about Maria's and Otto's status for the competition. The skaters arrived at the rink Saturday morning with toasted bagels, muffins, and whatever light fare they could eat before their skating events.

To everyone's amazement, Otto and Maria walked into the rink. A rush of caring friends and competitors asked frantically, "Are you okay? Are you dropping out?"

The Jelineks explained that Otto had suffered a concussion, but had received clearance from hospital doctors that morning to skate. They hadn't been sure the doctors would sign off, but they had, just in time.

Ladies and mens figures, along with compulsory ice dances, came first. The bleachers were filled to capacity with local skaters and their families. None of the top men performed figures that would be considered worthy of a world gold medal, but there were some standout moments, such as one of Bradley Lord's figures, called a "rocker." Writers described it as "outstanding."

Laurence substantially improved upon the figures she had done at U.S. Nationals. Maribel stood on the sidelines nodding in relief and approval as Laurence managed each maneuver with a confidence she hadn't shown before. Wendy was the clear second-place finisher. However, Laurence fumbled her last figure, the paragraph loop, missing the move entirely. The audience gasped. Laurence's lead was now cut to 5/10ths of a point. Maribel buried her head in her hands in disbelief.

Steffi, who had beaten Laurence in figures at Nationals, performed a surprisingly tentative set. She was placed fourth after the compulsories and was extremely upset with herself. Sherri rubbed Steffi's shoulders and assured her she could mount a comeback in the free skate. Edi, always wearing the instructor's hat, gave her tips that would help her improve at Worlds. Steffi knew that without a medal at the North Americans, the World judges would not take her as seriously in Prague. After all, if she couldn't even win a medal out of the seven best women in North America, how could she win a medal when facing more than twenty-five other women from other nations? She had to do an outstanding job in the free skate to make an impression. The pressure was monumental.

Maribel, ever the perfectionist, reminded Laurence that she needed to skate spectacularly to beat Wendy Griner, a skater known for her polish and exceptional double jumps. Laurence was distressed over flubbing the final figure in her first round, and she was eager to perform well in the free skate.

By Sunday morning, nerves jittered at full force. As with Nationals, cameras would record the event for broadcast, but it would be shown exclusively on a local Philadelphia television station. Canadian television also sent a cameraman to document the event. More than four thousand spectators crowded into the seats for the final day of competition.

Dee Dee Sherbloom and Larry Pierce kicked off the first event, ice dance. They performed much more smoothly than at Nationals, but the judges were not as kind this time. Their kicks, some surmised, were too high, and they suffered some slight miscues on their timing. They had a long wait before they'd know the results. Robert and Patricia Dineen were the next American dance team to perform. They skated quite well, but the biggest criticism of their style was that they skated too far apart from each other. They lacked the physical closeness that creates a more harmonious appearance.

The final American dancers were Dona Lee Carrier and Roger Campbell. In glittering black, they showed a command of edges and elegant transitions during the tempo changes in their music.

When the scores were tallied, only one American team had placed on the medal stand, and that was Dona Lee and Roger. Larry and Dee Dee finished a disappointing fourth, and Pat and Robert Dineen placed sixth out of six teams. As anticipated, Canadians Virginia Thompson and William McLachlan took the gold.

The first of the American ladies to skate was Karen Howland, who was still recovering from her flight to Philadelphia when she took to the ice for her free skate. Overall, her content was much simpler than what the other ladies were doing. She chose less difficult jumps and spins, and she fell twice.

Steffi was next. Wearing a red sparkling costume brand new for the event, she attacked her jumps, never losing her concentration the way she did at Nationals. She did have one fall, on a double loop. Some skaters consider themselves "toe jumpers," meaning they like the jumps that require jamming the toe pick into the ice to propel the skater into the air. Other jumpers consider themselves "edge jumpers," meaning they like those jumps that rely on pressure on a particular edge for the takeoff. The double loop is an edge jump, and Steffi seemed a much more confident toe jumper. Her spins were solid, but some of the Canadian skaters executed better ones. Again, she seemed irritated with herself following her performance, but overall, it was a much better effort than at Nationals. If she could put the complete package of figures and a free skate together at Worlds, she still had a chance at a medal.

Wendy Griner of Canada was next. Considered Laurence's biggest competition, Wendy had performed somewhat inconsistently in international competition, but when she skated a clean program, her flow and elegance were breathtaking. She had a light, delicate style that was very easy to watch—never jerky or

AP Images

Laurence, Maribel, and Mara pose happily after a final practice session before leaving for the North American championships.

frantic. She landed every double beautifully, but tripped when she followed a double flip jump directly with a sit spin in sequence. She never lost her timing, and the fall didn't seem like much of a distraction when it was over.

Laurence skated fourth in the group of seven ladies. Dressed in her lime green draped costume, she once again looked electric as she dashed onto the ice with her welcoming smile. She dazzled the crowd with large, high double jumps that appeared much stronger than at Nationals. She had a slight wobble on the landing of one of her double Axels, but she recovered without losing her timing to the music. Her spins, by all accounts, were the best of all the competitors.

When the ladies competition concluded, Laurence had secured her most impressive victory yet—she won the gold. Wendy Griner won the silver in a very close finish. Steffi just missed the podium, finishing in fourth. Just like her mother had been in 1934, Laurence was a North American champion. She sealed her reputation now as the top American lady skater, and her star was rising. Myra said that someone told her in confidence after the U.S. Nationals that Steffi was the winner over Laurence, but because of Big Maribel's name and connections, Laurence was "given" the championship. The North Americans put all doubt about Laurence's status to rest.

Dick Button, who was commentating for the local broadcast, interviewed a glowing Laurence after the event.

When Dick asked her how she felt, she just said, "I feel pretty good. After skating in the high altitude of Colorado Springs, this time it was easier to run my program."

Dick said to her, "Your mother is quite charming."

"Thank you. During my program I saw my mother hopping up and down. I think she was working harder than I was."

Another reporter interviewed Laurence, who was eager to fly to Prague, but still fretting over the slight bobble on her double Axel.

"I never had any trouble on the double Axel on which I slipped before this. I'm still thrilled and excited about winning. Yet, before I have a chance to calm down we'll be leaving tomorrow by plane for Prague. We're due to arrive sometime Wednesday."

Karen Howland finished seventh out of seven skaters, and still wondered if she'd be making the trip to Prague or if Rhode would recover in time to go.

For the Owen family, there was hardly time to celebrate. The pairs free skate was next, and the crowd and skaters were anxious to know how Maria and Otto would perform after such a frightening incident. Would his headache be gone? Would he become dizzy because of the concussion?

The Jelineks skated near the end of the flight, so they watched Dud and Mara and shouted encouragement from the side of the rink. Dressed in what Mara considered her "lucky" gold dress with brown fur trim, they skated well, clearly having fun as they managed the successful completion of each jump, spin, and lift. The crowd thunderously applauded them, and they left the ice beaming and hoping a medal was within their grasp.

Maria and Otto came next. The audience held its collective breath. The Jelineks were known as powerful skaters. On this particular night, they elected to slow down and skate more deliberately. Though they didn't attack the program with their usual fire, the performance was clean. In the final analysis, Otto and Maria had won the gold, and Mara and Dud were pleased to receive the silver behind their close friends. Maribel had hoped both her daughters could again bring home two gold medals, but the superiority of the Jelineks in the pairs event was without question. Americans Ila Ray and Ray Hadley finished just off the podium in fourth. Bill and Laurie Hickox finished last, a testament to their youth and need for polish on the ice. Seeing this event must have been a tremendous motivation for the younger skaters.

The finale again belonged to the men. Despite their lackluster performance in the school figures, the quality of the men's free skating was never in doubt. Don Jackson was a reigning Olympic bronze medalist and had a special flair to his skating. In the free skate, he was always striving to push the technical limits. He had been working on a triple Lutz—a jump that had never been performed by anyone. He did not plan to do that jump here, but the crowd was always eager to see what the exceptional Canadian would do next.

Don skated with ease and brilliance. He had a magnificent spring to his jumps. His program was flawless and full of panache. The Americans would have a difficult time matching him. Bradley Lord performed just as well in his routine, but he lacked the spark and artistry that Don had achieved. Gregory Kelley possessed strong artistry but sometimes had less than desirable air positions in his jumps. Still, he did have one triple jump in his arsenal—the Salchow—but he was not sure enough about it to bring it to this competition. He performed a solid routine and seemed to be a good prospect for a medal.

While Don took the gold, Bradley the silver, and Gregory the bronze, the night really belonged to the tiny dynamo from Detroit. Doug Ramsay had trouble in the school figures again, and seemed a long shot for a medal. But in the free skate his performance seemed effortless, charming the audience at every step. The young girls in the bleachers went crazy for his sweet smile, and ability to reach out to the audience in the most inviting way. The *Skating* magazine report did not offer nearly the accolades to other skaters as it did to Douglas:

> Douglas Ramsay was the darling of the audience. The foot stamping, applauding crowd acclaimed his every dextrous motion. His magnificent Axel with arms folded, and his skillful bracket dance brought loud cheers. The captivating Ramsay unfortunately missed a double Axel. He ended in fourth place.

AP Images

Douglas Ramsay was known as a showstopper. He is seen here after winning the 1960 Midwestern regional men's title.

Throughout the competition, the hotel phone operator was quite busy. The Westerfeld girls called Myra at home in Colorado every night, eager to share the exploits from the day. On the evening after the ladies event, Sherri placed the call so Steffi would not hear any initial disappointment in Myra's voice. It was in Sherri's personality to be protective of Steffi. The girls knew Myra was glued to the phone all day, waiting for it to ring with news. Sherri wanted to emphasize to Myra what Steffi had done in her program that was better than before. Sherri always wanted to focus on the positive. She held a consistent note of cheer in her voice, even as Myra let out a sad sigh. "Was the judging fair?" she probably asked. Steffi knew that she simply had to find that one, elusive, clean routine. Only then could a true comparison be made between her and Laurence.

Long-distance calls were not inexpensive, so conversations were kept to only a few minutes. The girls told their mother they loved and missed her, to kiss Seric, and that they'd call from the New York airport on Tuesday.

The Philadelphia Skating Club and Humane Society would

now convert from competition venue to party spot. A superb fete was planned, giving all the skaters time to bond even more within a no-pressure situation. A buffet line was formed, and the young men and women crammed the food into their bodies quickly so they could dance off the pent-up stress of the competition. The pairs skaters demonstrated how their skills could translate marvelously onto the dance floor, with lifts set in time to the music. The heat generated on the dance floor was a drastic change from the bitter cold outside. The crowd roared in laughter as Maribel was dragged from her chair onto the dance floor, where they demanded that she dance. She resisted as best she could, finally relenting and twitching her hips in the most uncomfortable and out-of-fashion way. The frolickers howled in appreciation of her efforts. The party went on until two in the morning. One final dance slowed the pace. Young gentleman skaters asked the young ladies who had retreated to their chairs, "May I have this dance?"

Dud pulled a sleepy Mara close to him, their cheeks touching and his hot breath warming her face. They danced in time to the music—no fear of tripping, falling, or being dropped. It was just one relaxing dance to unite them. The doting look in Dud's eyes beckoned Mara's inner hopes. "Could this be the moment he asks?" They talked about getting married and starting a family quite openly, but Mara had no idea when the question would come. Deep in her heart, she knew it must be Prague. The mysterious, gothic, forbidden world that was hidden to most Westerners would be such an enchanting place to become engaged. Her mother would have preferred her focus to be on the important World Championships, but Mara preferred, at least for this quiet, perfect moment on the dance floor, to drift off to her dreams of romance and a new life under the same roof as the man she loved, a partner in a every endeavor, a dream that took her to the day of her wedding, the day when she'd vow eternal love to her dapper Dud, until death do them part.

Chapter Nine

"Laurence, hurry up or we're leaving without you!" Maribel called out to her daughter impatiently. The silver bus idled in front of the hotel as the New York-bound passengers handed their luggage to the cigar-smoking, bolo-hatted driver. Laurence was still struggling to get her arms into her coat sleeves when she made her way outside.

"My youngest daughter has no sense of time," Maribel vented.

This was quite true. Laurence, for all her stellar scholarly work, was always the last out of bed, the last to finish her breakfast, and the last to have her skates laced before the warm-ups. Today, at least, she was first out of bed, along with Dud, but found other ways to make herself late. The driver took Laurence's tardy additions to the cargo hold and pressed them into the last nook available before slamming the door. The driver skipped up the steps of the bus and waited for the Owens to finish one last bit of business before all the skaters would depart for New York. Their dear friend from the Boston Club had received word that her mother would require surgery. Instead of officiating at the World Championships as planned, Mary Louise Wright informed Laurence and Mara she'd be unable to join them on their global adventure.

"I have to care for my mother in Minneapolis," she said. "But I'll be thinking about you."

Laurence stuck out her bottom lip and tried to guilt her about not coming, and in a pretend bratty voice said, "I am temporarily mad at you."

Mary Louise smiled as she embraced her for a hug.

"I promise I'll go with you next year. Skate your best."

Laurence and Mara filed into the bus, where Maribel and Dud had saved them seats. Maribel instantly commanded the attention of her troops to go over the itinerary hour by hour, but Laurence was more interested in her cheese and crackers.

The mood was rambunctious, although the more quiet members of the team, such as Bradley Lord, were content to soak in their surroundings as towns clicked by outside the bus windows. Douglas Ramsay and his coach, Bill Swallender, hadn't even planned to be on this bus, but what a wonderful experience they were having. If Doug could just perform solidly in his school figures, they surmised, he would be as big a hit with the judges as he was with the audience.

The most relieved passenger of all must have been Rhode Michelson. Her badly bruised hip had responded well to the ice packs and the three days of rest. Just to be sure, while the other skaters, coaches, and chaperones went shopping during their extra day in Philadelphia, she and coach Bill Kipp held a training session on the lonely patch of ice where championships had been decided the night before. Bill eased Rhode into the workout. She first did some crossovers, followed by a few simple single jumps, with the occasional school figure thrown in for good measure. Bill, not wanting her to risk re-injuring the hip, would not let her do any double jumps, although she was tempted. The thrill of performing a multi-revolution jump is quite intoxicating. Bill and Rhode were confident, though, that she would handle the doubles in Prague.

Karen Rowland, the alternate who gallantly filled in on short notice, was told she'd be going home. She must have felt dejected as the jubilant American team boarded the bus and sped off without her.

Aboard the bus, someone remarked that it was Valentine's Day. Mara and Dud, along with Pat and Bob Dineen, were the resident lovebirds on the bus, and they nuzzled close to generate some warmth. Everyone was bundled in their best traveling clothes and coats. Riding in an airplane at that time was a formal event. The young men wore blazers, dress slacks, and ties. The ladies wore skirts and dress shoes. They wore dress coats with fur collars. Maribel, never one to care much about fashion (and certainly someone who never had time to shop), was wearing the same hunter green velvet, feather-tipped hat she had been wearing for several years. The hat had begun to show its age, but Maribel had bigger things to worry about.

The Westerfeld girls worked on Steffi's homework. This trip would bring to five the number of weeks of school missed because of Steffi's extracurricular activities. That was simply unheard of in those days. Steffi was fortunate to have a very understanding principal at Cheyenne Mountain High School who allowed her to work ahead in anticipation of these trips and events.

One school was not as understanding. Junior national champion Lorraine Hanlon was invited to go on the trip to perform in the European exhibitions. Lorraine's ultimate goal was to attend Harvard Medical School. To attain a Harvard-level pedigree, Lorraine was required to attend a top-notch academy before college. She attended the prestigious Windsor School in Boston, and school leaders felt skating was a distraction from academics that could not be tolerated. The school gave Lorraine a choice: skating or Windsor. Their exact words were "If you go to Prague, find another school when you come back." As the bus departed, Lorraine was at home in Boston contemplating her next move.

She was extremely close to some of the competitors, and this would be a journey full of fun. She could remember all the times she had spent with her skating friends, but one stood out as the stuff of legend. Lorraine once invited Laurence along to the beach with her family. A recent hurricane had produced a dangerous undertow, and Lorraine's mother forbade them to go into the water. When she turned her back, Laurence decided she wanted to swim. The other kids couldn't stop her—she was too stubborn. Laurence proceeded into the strong current. The other kids were worried, but followed her as she swam around. Then they realized they were watching someone else. They scanned the beach a dozen times and realized that Laurence was nowhere to be found. They ran for the lifeguards.

After more than an hour, search parties were called in. A helicopter flew overhead. Two hours later, searchers were dragging the water for her. Still nothing. Lorraine and her mother wept, and wondered aloud how they would tell Big Maribel.

All hope seemed to be lost. But then, about four hours later, Laurence came walking barefoot down the road. She had landed on a neighboring beach. Lorraine recalled of that day, "My mother nearly strangled her."

Laurence slid deeper into her window seat aboard the bus and wondered what Lorraine had decided to do about her trip. Laurence also wondered something else: "Is my *Sports Illustrated* for sale yet?"

Just before the Owens had departed for the North American Championships, Barbara Heilman, a reporter for *Sports Illustrated* magazine, had come to their Boston home, photographer in tow. Because outdoor lighting was so much better than what the Boston skating rinks could provide, the Owens were beckoned to an outdoor pond flanked by trees as tall as cathedrals. Laurence was asked to don a skating dress similar to what she'd wear at a competition. Maribel wasn't so sure, concerned Laurence would catch a cold before her most important competitions. The photographer promised the shoot would go quickly, and Maribel relented. Laurence smiled brilliantly for the camera, her cheeks rosy from the rush of winter air. She clearly enjoyed the attention she was receiving.

The reporter, photographer, and Owen women returned to High Street for an interview. Maribel resisted the temptation to lend her journalistic advice to the reporter, who asked a series of questions while the photographer took candid shots of Laurence and Maribel sifting through the fan mail that had just arrived in the mailbox. The reporter asked a fascinating question.

"Mrs. Owen, do you consider yourself a better skater than Laurence?"

Maribel answered, "I could surely beat Laurence in the school figures, but in the free skate, Laurence would beat me handily."

On the bus to the airport, Laurence suddenly remembered that the issue would be hitting newsstands right before the trip to Worlds.

After the two-and-a-half hour trip to New York's Idlewild Airport (mockingly referred to as "Idle Rich" by locals), the bus parked at the curb near the international terminal where the team checked in for their ten-hour flight to Brussels.

A Sabena representative assisted them with their baggage and the passport inspections. The group was led down a long hallway of tall glass windows to the lounge, where they were served tea, coffee, Coca-Cola, and small snacks. The lounge allowed some to catch up on business before the trip.

United States Figures Skating Association President F. Ritter Shumway, installed to the presidency only after the sudden fatal heart attack of predecessor Howard Herbert (to whom the 1961 Nationals was dedicated), was nervous about the first major international event since the Nationals. He wanted to go, but

AP Images

Laurence, Maribel, Mara, and Dudley gather on the tarmac minutes before boarding the plane to Brussels.

business at headquarters since Herbert's death demanded that he stay behind. The ordained minister, ice dancer, and wealthy philanthropist (his father had invented the Ritter dental chair) instead watched from a distance. On the evening the flight left, he became simultaneously sullen and fidgety. He had an irrepressible urge to call the airport and make sure everything was okay. He sent a Western Union message to the airport shortly before departure time.

"Best wishes to all for interesting and successful trip. Please ask Walter Powell to phone me before departure. –Ritter"

Walter received the message and called Ritter in short order, reassuring him that everything was on schedule, and that everyone was in good spirits.

Ritter hung up the phone and told his secretary, "I had a terrible feeling talking to them to just now. I can't explain it."

An hour before takeoff, ice dancer Bob Dineen dashed to the 50th Street Skate Shop in New York City to have his blades sharpened one last time before the trip. He and Pat had driven to the North American Championships and were able to go home following their event. His friend Steve Witizen was behind the counter and reminded Bob that he didn't like to be rushed. "Bobby," he said, "why don't you take your time and catch another plane?" Moments later, the job was finished—Bob and Pat Dineen would make their flight after all.

Lorraine Hanlon, just a few hours before she needed to leave, made a painful decision. She simply couldn't risk expulsion from her school to skate in an exhibition. She was going to abandon the trip. She unpacked her luggage and stayed, broken-hearted, in Boston.

At the airport, it didn't take long for Mara and Dud to spot their Canadian friends, Maria and Otto Jelinek. Together, they traded with some other passengers so they could ride with the Americans and be more relaxed about traveling to their native country. One of the trade recipients was Walter Powell.

Traveling behind the Iron Curtain was unique, but the eighty-one-year-old Powell had done it before and was in no way anxious about the flight. He was scheduled to be the referee at Worlds. A shoe company executive from St. Louis, he was a longtime skater whose wealth afforded him a travel budget that made him a popular choice to officiate at major events.

Maria and Otto called their parents to alert them about the trade. They would now be passengers on Sabena Flight 548.

Bruce Hyland was the Jelineks' coach. Bruce's wife had just given birth that evening, and he was already exhausted, yet overjoyed. His mood turned slightly sour when, after speaking with Maria and Otto, he learned they were traveling with the Americans. Hyland put his foot down.

"This is ridiculous," he said. "You are Canadians and will travel with the Canadian team."

Hyland was the boss, and despite minor protestations from Otto, the matter was closed. The Jelineks delivered the bad news to their American friends that they would simply have to meet again in Prague. The two couples fondly embraced and then parted.

Larry Pierce and Dee Dee Sherbloom were already regretting an earlier decision. The two-foot-tall silver trophy they were given for winning the Nationals was becoming cumbersome. Larry thought it would be a great source of motivation, so he had brought it with him. He was already sick of carrying it, and Dee Dee wasn't interested in holding it either. Fortunately, Sabena offered to ship it back to Indianapolis so it would be waiting for him when he returned. The trophy would stay with him for the first half of the year before Dee Dee took it. Larry was relieved that his baggage load was now lighter.

Larry and Dee Dee's coach, Daniel Ryan, a devout Roman Catholic, called his wife, Rose Anne, one last time before boarding Sabena Flight 548. He had a few simple and loving requests. "Promise me three things—that you will go to church, always keep smiling, and take care of yourself."

Steffi and Sherri called Myra one last time, too. Myra was biting her nails down to the stubs over the prospect of her little girls flying over the ocean to a foreign, communist land. Her voice choked as she bid farewell to the girls, who were also overcome with emotion and excitement.

Laurence glanced over her shoulder and noticed a small newsstand.

"There it is!" she exclaimed. She tugged her mother away from an ongoing conversation and the two gushed over what they saw. A ravishing Laurence, clad in a bright red dress and gliding backward on a pond wearing her famously big smile, was on the cover of

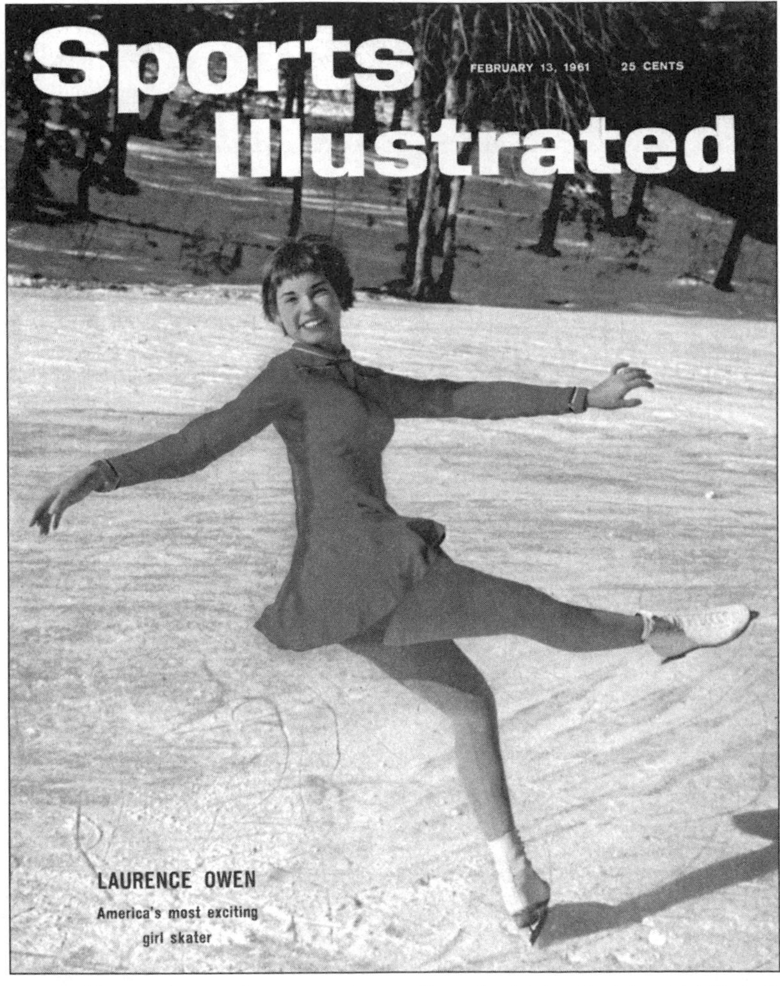

Photo courtesy of *Sports Illustrated*

Sports Illustrated named Laurence Owen "America's Most Exciting Girl Skater" in the issue on stands the day the team departed for Prague.

Sports Illustrated. The headline read "Laurence Owen: America's Most Exciting Girl Skater." Maribel bought several copies and they planned to read the article on the plane. The other skaters were impatient to see it. One can only imagine how this lavish praise of Laurence must have hurt Steffi, who had come so close to being America's number-one girl skater. If Steffi possessed any teenage jealously at all, she remained poised throughout the fussing over Laurence.

The plane they would soon be boarding was a Boeing 707 jet. The 707 was referred to in magazine ads and posters as "America's first jetliner," but that was really a misstatement of the facts. While its success did bring about the "Jet Age" and was the first of Boeing's 7x7 range of aircraft, the distinction of first commercial jetliner belonged to the De Havilland Comet. That plane was plagued with midair mechanical failures, and the entire fleet was even grounded once. It barely beat the 707 in the race to become the first commercial jet to fly a transatlantic flight.

The first prototype of the 707, the Boeing 367-80, also called the "Dash 80," was developed in 1952. From this design came the 707. The fuselage was widened by six inches from the original design to accommodate six-abreast passenger seating, and it featured a wingspan of 130 feet.

The Boeing 707 was considered the most state-of-the-art passenger plane to date. Not a single Boeing 707 had ever been involved in a fatal crash. This revolutionary plane, if one was to believe the press attention it received, was beginning to get the same naïve "unsinkable" reputation as the famed ocean liner *Titanic*.

The plane could hold eighty-nine passengers. The passenger area was divided into two sections, first class and economy class. The cockpit was equipped with seating for a captain, a first officer, and a second officer.

The first airline to purchase and fly the 707 was Pan Am. Belgian flagship carrier Sabena and Air France became the first foreign carriers to order the planes in bulk. Sabena purchased seven and took delivery of a model 707-329, serial number 17624/92/ registration OO-SJB, in 1960. On February 14, 1961, this plane, now tagged as Sabena Flight 548, had logged 3,038 flight hours, which in airline language was just about brand new.

AP Images

Standing on tarmac, left to right: Deane McMinn (team manager), Laurence Owen, Douglas Ramsay, Steffi Westerfeld, Gregory Kelley, Rhode Michelson, Bradley Lord.
First row, plane steps: Maribel Y. Owen, Dudley Richards.
Second row, plane steps: Bill Hickox, Ray Hadley.
Third row, plane steps: Laurie Hickox, Larry Pierce, Ila Ray Hadley.
Fourth row, plane steps: Roger Campbell, Diane Sherbloom.
Fifth row, plane steps: Dona Lee Carrier.
Sixth row, plane steps: Robert Dineen.
Seventh row, plane steps: Patricia Dineen.

The American skating delegation would not be alone on the flight. Many other passengers were aboard—business executives, military personnel, military wives, a young pregnant woman, and even a priest.

The anticipation was building and hearts were racing as the passengers were rounded up into the boarding area. They were escorted on a bus to runway #22R. The entire thirty-four-member U.S. figure skating entourage started filing up the steps of the plane, bundled in their traveling coats. On their lapels they wore the special commemorative pins minted for the Worlds meet.

The atmosphere was electric as they moved closer to the door of the plane, but the call "Wait!" shot from the tarmac below. An Associated Press photographer wanted to capture this triumphant moment on film for the morning papers. Deane McMinn, the team manager, rearranged everyone according to who he felt should be more center stage in the photos. On the far left, Deane held up a white cardboard sign that read, "U.S. Figure Skating Association." Ladies champion Laurence Owen was to his left, and sported the large and warm smile for which she had become famous. Steffi occupied the desirable middle front of the photograph, and Rhode was off to her right. The men's champions filed behind them, some with their feet on the ground, and others half-perched on the stairs to the plane. The next rows were a mélange of pairs teams and ice dancers. Larry Pierce, near the top of the stairs, held up all five fingers—to signal the middle finger times five, a joke he knew his good friend Ron Ludington would especially appreciate when he saw the next morning's sports section. The flashbulbs popped, capturing the glowing faces of the U.S. team.

With a photographer's "thank you and bon voyage," the skaters trampled up the stairs, medals bouncing on their chests, and lucky silver dollars jangling in a few pockets.

Chapter Ten

Not a soul survives who can possibly know what took place inside the cabin of Sabena Flight 548 as the skaters, coaches, officials, and loved ones took their seats aboard the doomed aircraft. We can only imagine the nervousness that would be part of the first-ever transatlantic flying experience for some, the conversations that likely took place, and the inner thoughts and fears the passengers carried with them on board. We can only use our imaginations—based on what we know about the passengers—to fill in the gaps of the last moments of their lives in this account of the events on board.

Complete silence fell over the cabin as Sabena Flight 548 prepared for takeoff. Even the most veteran travelers like Maribel sat in silence. The five male stewards and two female flight hostesses, wearing their crisp white uniforms with the curvy blue "S" on their nametags, had completed their pre-flight instructions. Hostess Jacqueline Trullemans helped demonstrate the proper way to fasten seatbelts. She cheerfully explained the correct crash position. In her Belgian-French accent, she explained the position was, "Head down between the knees, hands over the head." Some of the passengers even practiced the maneuver with her.

Mara was visibly uncomfortable with the demonstration and turned to Dudley, who offered some words of comfort. She slid her small hand into his. He gripped her hand tightly as they both surveyed the plane for the emergency exits as instructed by the flight crew.

Laurence sat with her mother, and both were fully engrossed in the *Sports Illustrated* article that had made Laurence the resident celebrity of the plane. Laurence read the article's title out loud for her sister and Dud to hear, too: "Mother set the style. Pretty Laurence Owen is the most exciting U.S. skater, but in her remarkable family she is just another champion."

They all grinned with approval and planned to dive deeper into the article after takeoff. Big Maribel wondered to herself how her sinuses would react when the plane reached altitude. She had broken her nose in an accident before Nationals, when a bakery truck slammed into her car. She was suing the Apollo Cake Specialties bakery for $15,000 as a result of the problems she had been having since the accident.

Seated several rows behind the Owen family were Steffi and Sherri Westerfeld. In their hands, travel brochures and pamphlets about Prague and other European destinations greatly excited them.

Steffi's coach, Edi Scholdan, was doing his best to put on a brave front for his son, James. Edi hated flying, and was trying to accentuate the positive—the return to his homeland of Austria following Worlds.

Larry Pierce, Danny Ryan, and Dee Dee Sherbloom sat across the aisle. Larry must have beamed with gratitude at Dee Dee, without whom he would not be a national champion, and he would not be taking this exciting trip. Danny was preoccupied with his wife, Rose Anne, and their big family. Fortunately, Rose Anne's parents had journeyed from Canada to Indianapolis to help. They were even going to take some of the kids back to Canada so Rose

Anne wouldn't have her hands too full with the new baby.

The time for takeoff had arrived. The plane rolled to its mark on the night-darkened runway and was still for just a few minutes. The pilot, Louis Lambrechts, did a final check of the plane's controls, assisted by his first officer Jean Roy.

Captain Lambrechts, at age forty-four, was somewhat a legend in Belgium. He was a decorated war hero for his courageous flying with the British Royal Air Force in World War II. He was knighted by the King of Belgium and was honored by the British and French governments. It was only natural that he should take the reigns as a senior pilot with Belgium's flagship carrier, which was a symbol of national pride, ingenuity, and financial standing.

Captain Lambrechts had completed his certification to fly Boeing 707 aircraft, day or night, on February 27, 1960. He was given what the Belgian Ministry of Communications calls a "proficiency check" on October 17, 1960, and he was due for a license renewal on July 30, 1961. He had logged 840 hours of flying time on the aircraft, as much as one could expect for a plane in service for less than a decade.

The plane began rolling for a few seconds at moderate speed, followed by a distinct acceleration that set hearts racing. Some passengers tightly closed their eyes. As the plane tilted upward, some people clutched their stomachs, or the armrests, or the hand of a loved one. Second by second, the brightly lit New York skyline became smaller and smaller, before the winter clouds blocked the ground from view altogether.

The cabin's darkness allowed many to sleep as comfortably as possible in such a cramped cabin. A few passengers conversed softly but mostly a silence pervaded the plane until, hours later, the sun beamed through the windows. Land came into view just enough for the passengers to see the fabled white cliffs of Dover.

As dawn gave way to morning, the stewards served a breakfast of French toast (known to the Europeans as "pain a farine"), fruit, and juice or coffee to the passengers. The clank of sterling silverware converted the aircraft into a restaurant in the sky.

As the plane crossed into the northern portion of France, the pilot announced, "Today there will be a total eclipse of the sun visible shortly."

Everyone debated whether or not it was really unsafe to view the eclipse, and if they could take pictures of it. Some cautious passengers pulled down their window shades. Darkness came again as the moon obstructed the sun's view, creating a black circle with a ring of fire around it. The spectacular event lasted nearly three minutes.

The pilot then informed the passengers the temperature was unseasonably warm in Brussels, hovering in the mid-forties. The stewards made their way up and down the aisles to collect dirty plates and trash.

Belgium then came in to view. Wulpen. Mackel. Dender. The passengers would not have known the names of the small Belgian towns over which they were flying, but those by the windows strained to see anyway. The towns must have seemed both quaint and exotic to the eyes of the Americans, most of whom had never been across the ocean. The voices of the young passengers grew louder with their excitement at arriving in Europe.

Some of the Americans pulled cameras from their carry-on baggage. Shutters snapped furiously, camera lenses pressed against the thick windows that preserved the airtight, pressurized atmosphere aboard Sabena Flight 548. The ten-hour flight was nearing its end. Laurence squinted to capture the hint of humanity on the ground just a few thousand feet below the aircraft. Visibility was perfect as the bright morning sun illuminated the enchanting cottages, their thatched rooftops beckoning as the plane reached lower and lower to the earth.

As the plane descended, the roar of the four Pratt and Whitney JT4A turbojet engines would have been apparent to the farmers and workers in the small forest enclave of Berg, a town within the municipality of Kampenhout, just outside of Brussels. Several Berg residents later claimed they could see the passengers taking pictures of the ground and waving to people below.

Captain Lambrechts began the plane's final descent, aiming toward runway twenty at Brussels International Airport. As he prepared for final descent, the tower informed him he would need to make a slight modification to his flight plan, since a small plane had just landed on Sabena 548's runway, and would need to clear the way. Captain Lambrechts was asked to circle the area twice before his final approach.

The passengers were a little confused, but Captain Lambrechts calmly informed them of the slight change. Suddenly, the chatter aboard the plane stopped. Mara again sported a worried face. Dud assured her this was a normal maneuver, and there was no need to be concerned. The tower then logged this communication with the cockpit.

Pilot: "Estimating Brussels-Aircraft technically O.K."

Tower: "Roger... runway 20 for landing, the wind 330 degrees/2 kt, if you wish I'll take you for final approach."

Pilot: "Roger. Thank you."

Tower: "What's your heading now?"

Pilot: "Heading 10... [hesitation] 110."

Tower: "Roger. Take the heading of 080 to the left."

Pilot: "Roger. 080."

The communication between the tower and the aircraft was silent for three minutes, until the tower again initiated contact with Sabena Flight 548.

Tower: "Identified 13 N.M. WNW... continue on your heading and also your descent."

Pilot: "Roger."

Tower: "Present level and rate of descent?"

Pilot: "We have to reduce speed to make a quick descent, we are now descending thousand feet a minute. We expect to go south as soon..."

Tower: "What's your present level?"

Pilot: "10,000 feet descending."

Tower: "In that case will you turn left heading 020."

Pilot: "Roger. 020."

Tower: "You are coming too close to the antenna. I will lose sight of you on the radar."

Pilot: "Roger."

The tower would never again hear from the pilots.

Captain Lambrechts could see the tower, where his wife was waiting to greet him after the completion of yet another lengthy shift. When the plane descended to 600 feet, the captain lowered the landing gear. The passengers, nervous about the circling pattern, relaxed again. It appeared they would be safely on the ground in less than a minute. The runway was close. Then the passengers were violently shaken from their thoughts.

Captain Lambrechts pulled up the landing gear and fought to aim the plane's nose back into the sky. The control tower tried to contact the cockpit several times.

"Tower to Sabena 548, do you read? Repeat, Sabena 548 do you read?"

Air traffic controllers heard only dead air as the captain's and first officer's hands quivered in a frantic fight with the plane's steering devices. The plane zigzagged in the air, shaking violently, its engines growling. It banked sharply to the left, heading higher, until witnesses say the plane was pointing straight up. The passengers were either screaming or couldn't catch their breaths to scream. One can only dare imagine the chaos inside the cabin. As they'd been instructed at takeoff, the passengers lowered their heads between their knees and put their hands over their heads. Maintaining this position was difficult because the plane kept tossing them from side to side, the seatbelts squeezing their stomachs.

The plane appeared to hit a virtual ceiling when it could climb and turn no more.

It went into what pilots call a "Dutch roll," its left wing tipping over and sending the plane's nose into a collision course with the ground. The pilot and copilot fought to bring the plane level again, but it continued its fall to earth, turning in a helix until it crushed into a cabbage field. The plane exploded then disintegrated only 1,200 feet from the runway. The white-hot flames burned clothing off the bodies of the passengers.

The time was 9:05 a.m. From the moment the trouble first became evident, thirty seconds had passed. Thirty seconds during which entire lives flickered in the passengers' minds like an old tragic movie—only in this film, they were the stars—the tragic figures withering like flowers in the most helpless of scenarios. A final "I love you" may have been shared between those mothers and daughters, husbands and wives, young lovers, and closest of siblings. Perhaps someone stated what was already understood: "This is it. We're all going to die."

Just minutes before the peace was broken, twenty-four-year-old Theo Delaet was tending to his cabbage field. Delaet, a Belgian amateur cyclist, could hear that something was amiss, and he craned his neck to see the source of the sound. Perhaps he was blinded by the morning sun, or perhaps he simply could not run fast enough, but a heavy piece of flaming debris found Delaet's very spot, killing him instantly, bringing Sabena Flight 548's death toll up to seventy-three. Another field worker, twenty-seven-year-old Marcel Lauwers, was also struck by debris, and he lost a leg.

Sabena had just earned the tragic distinction of being the first airline to lose a 707 jetliner. The inquest into what went wrong began with many obvious questions. Why did Captain Lambrechts retract the landing gear? Would the plane have landed safely without having been required to circle the area twice? Why was another plane on Flight 548's runway so close to its scheduled landing time?

The questions would never be answered clearly. Whatever the answers, the result was irreversible. Seventy-three people had perished. Thirty-four members of the U.S. skating delegation were dead. Ten of their families had lost two or three members. The dead included five sets of siblings, five groupings of a parent and child (or children), and two husband-and-wife couples. The United States figure skating program that had dominated at the three previous Olympics was now obliterated. The hopes and dreams of the skaters and coaches on board the aircraft had evaporated into the dense cloud of burning jet fuel. If there was one consolation to be found, it's that Captain Lambrechts seemingly carried out a final act of heroism for his countrymen. Witnesses reported that he seemed to be deliberately aiming the plane away from the small farming cottages that dotted the landscape, saving the lives of dozens of people.

In Berg Kampenhout, Belgium, the blare of fire truck sirens was heard even before the sound of the plane's impact thundered through the town. The control tower personnel, shadowed by Captain Lambrecht's wife, saw the plane's erratic maneuvers and called for emergency crews as they helplessly watched, perplexed and with a heavy sense of dread.

Fire crews rushed to the scene to douse the flames as they choked on the intense smell of burning jet fuel and charred human remains. It was instantly clear that no one had survived. A burned and whimpering German shepherd dog, whose crushed and melted kennel entombed him, was found under the wing next to two crushed bodies. A Belgian police officer put the dog out of its misery with a single bullet from his gun.

Stan Wayman/Time & Life Pictures/Getty Images

The wreckage of Sabena flight 548 near Brussels, Belgium.

The passenger list included eighteen champion American figure skaters, sixteen skating officials, coaches, and family members. There were twenty-seven other passengers and eleven crewmembers. The victims had struck a final and tragic pose in their seats, their hands over their heads, their bodies locked in the braced position. Most were still strapped in their seats, but they were burned beyond recognition.

The crash scene was strewn with body parts, burnt skating dresses, passports, suitcases, and shoes. Bodies had shattered like porcelain dolls. One of the only intact bodies was thirty-six-year-old Sabena flight attendant Jacqueline Trullemans. The scene was so horrific, veteran firefighters collapsed and were taken to the hospital.

A pair of melted ice skates dangled from the plane's aileron. The plane was broken into pieces rarely larger than a few feet wide. The largest recognizable piece was a jagged section of the tail, driven like a spear into the earth. A section of the wing was also jammed into the dirt, bearing the letter "S" in white paint.

A local priest rushed to his parish, grabbed some holy oils, and hurried back to bless the scene and perform the last rites on the passengers. In addition to the American skating entourage, the passengers included young brides, expectant mothers, a priest, restaurateurs, educators, and businessmen. Their names were eclipsed in the headlines by the American skaters.

Juanita Lemoine, who was married to an American Army private stationed in Europe, was on her first plane ride. As she hugged and kissed family members good-bye in New York, she told them, "I'm frightened to death."

She would have been in good company with Margaret Pozzuolo, who was only twenty years old, and carrying her first baby. Her husband was an American Army cook stationed in Germany.

Martin Soria was an associate professor of art history at Michigan State University. He was an authority on Spanish art and was on his way to be a guest lecturer in Europe.

Richard Robinson was a career U.S. Army officer, who was on Sabena Flight 548 with his Belgian bride, Jacqueline. They were returning to Belgium after getting married in the States.

Howard Lillie was the manager of research and development at Corning Glass Works. He was the president of the International Commission on Glass, which was meeting in Brussels.

Julian Baginski, thirty-three, of Englewood Cliffs, New Jersey, operated a restaurant called the Italian Pavilion. He was on his way to Warsaw, Poland, where his mother was dying of cancer.

And there was the Reverend Otmar Boesch of Seattle. For eighteen years, he served as a priest at Saint James Cathedral. He was taking his first vacation in five years, and he was meeting his parents in Brussels.

When Sabena Flight 548 crashed, some officials with the United States Figure Skating Association had already arrived in Europe—among them, the man who booked the American skaters' passage on the doomed plane.

H. Kendall Kelley and his wife were in Vienna, Austria. They had flown the day before the U.S. team departed. Kelley would have booked himself on Sabena Flight 548, but he was scheduled to judge at the World Championships and didn't want to spend too much time with the skaters to prevent any appearance of impropriety.

The new president of the USFSA broke the terrible news to the Kelleys in a late-night phone call to their Vienna hotel. F. Ritter Shumway had been the president of the U.S. Figure Skating Association for only a month. Now, he would carry the U.S. skating program through its darkest time.

Shumway requested that Kelley go to the scene to assist Belgian authorities in identifying victims and in communicating with grieving relatives in the States. He was unable to get an immediate flight from Vienna to Brussels, waiting an agonizing twelve more hours before he could secure an airplane to take him to that charred crater just outside Brussels.

As Kelley and his wife packed, they came across a program for the North American Championships, which featured pictures of the skaters. Kelley planned to give this document to Belgian officials in case it could help in identifying bodies.

When Kelley arrived in Belgium on February 16, he was joined by the president of the Skating Club of Boston, Edward Marshall. They met with Sabena officials and were given a tour of the Palais de Justice morgue where bodies were held. They were then given a tour of the scene, the wreckage still smoldering, the stench of death still thick. Almost nothing, save bodies and body parts, had been removed from the crash site.

A suitcase that presumably belonged to Laurence Owen caught Kelley's gaze. Inside, a blackened copy of the *Sports Illustrated* cover featuring Laurence lay peacefully in the debris, as if Laurence were smiling up at him. The scarf she wore as she boarded the flight had been stuffed into the suitcase with the magazine, and lay in the burned pile. Kelley caught a glimpse of Belgian royalty when King Badouin and Queen Fabiola visited to pay their respects. The queen held a handkerchief to her nose to try to block the pungent odor. The stoic queen finally broke down in the field of wreckage and was escorted away by her entourage.

Kelley brought U.S. Army Private Lemoine of New Orleans to the crash site. Lemoine's nineteen-year-old wife, Juanita, was "frightened to death" of flying. Kelley described Private Lemoine as "pitifully crushed in a maze of foreign language and red tape."

Kelley then began the grim task of contacting family members to request dental records that would help in the identification process. He discovered in this morose journey that bureaucracy was as much a part of death as grieving itself, as evidenced by the following letter written to F. Ritter Shumway. As of the date of this letter, February 23, 1961, only ten bodies connected to the U.S. skating program had been positively identified. One of those bodies was Dudley Richards. His identification was made easier by the fact that he was wearing his gold medal when the plane crashed. Kelley filled Shumway in on every pertinent detail.

"Sabena was providing oak caskets with heavy brass bolts and

Stan Wayman/Time & Life Pictures/Getty Images

A copy of Laurence Owen's *Sports Illustrated* cover is found in the wreckage of Sabena Flight 548.

hardware," Kelley wrote. "All (or most) are smaller than usual because of the conditions of the victims. Brass nameplates with dates of birth and death are affixed. On coffins of Protestants is a cross. On those of Catholics will be a crucifix with the body of Christ."

Stan Wayman/Time & Life Pictures/Getty Images

A burnt skate rests near an Olympic team jacket in the wreckage of Sabena Flight 548.

The wheels of bureaucracy sometimes perplexed Kelley, and dealing with the tedium no doubt brought additional pain to families. Sabena was in charge of processing death certificates, which could only be issued after all the bodies had been properly identified. Identifications were made using fingerprints when possible, large shreds of passports, and engraved wristwatches in some cases. The death certificates then had to be certified by the city of Berg. Sabena was legally required to obtain permission from Belgian authorities before releasing the bodies to the United States. Families were asked to supply the Belgian government with the addresses of funeral parlors in the appropriate cities. The U.S. Embassy in Brussels then had to approve the shipment of the bodies back to American soil. The only exception to this rule was the military personnel on the plane. Air Cadet William Hickox was, for this reason, the first of the U.S. skaters to make it home to his family. The body of Laurie, his sister and pairs partner, stayed behind. Lute and Elinor Hickox were forced to make two trips to greet their dead children as they returned to the United States.

Kelley informed Shumway in his morbidly detailed letter that Sabena would pay for all normal funeral expenses but not "for enclosing the bodies in heavy metal caskets or any elaborate ceremonies."

Kelley's final thought on the matter: "I feel it best I do not get into this with Sabena."

Chapter Eleven

Lorraine Hanlon was back in Boston, sound asleep. Instead of performing in ice shows in Europe, she would return to school. As she slept, a vivid nightmare erupted in her mind, a nightmare filled with images of fire.

Lorraine's name still appeared on the roster of those team members traveling abroad, and it was evident most believed she was on the plane, a fact made all the more obvious by the shrill sound of a ringing phone.

Mr. Hanlon answered, and on the line was the dispassionate voice of a newspaper reporter: "The plane has crashed. Your daughter is dead. Can we do an interview?" That surreal phone call triggered a conflicting shockwave of grief and relief in the Hanlon household. Dozens of friends were dead, but their daughter had been spared. The pendulum of fate had swung in this family's favor.

Lorraine, still unaware of flight 548's demise, was shaken from her dream-disturbed sleep by her mother, who charged up the stairs screaming, "They're all dead!"

On the morning of February 15, 1961, those words took on a new meaning. Phones, televisions, and messenger services all began to relay the tragic news as most North Americans poured their first cups of coffee.

One house with a lone old lady became a frenetic epicenter of grief with a ring of the doorbell. At 195 High Street in Winchester, Massachusetts, resided Gertrude "Granny" Vinson, the mother of Maribel Vinson Owen, and the proud grandmother of her newly crowned champion granddaughters, Laurence and Mara.

Mary Louise Wright, who had held a ticket for the doomed flight, was a friend to many of the plane's passengers. She recalled turning on the *Today* show with Dave Garroway around 7:00 a.m. when she heard the news. She said the next few weeks were a blur. She recalled one significant and sobering moment of February 15 more clearly than others. At 9:00 a.m., Wright's friends, including Dr. Hollis Albright, the father of Tenley Albright, Maribel Vinson Owen's student, were dispatched to Granny Vinson's home. Once inside, they explained to her that they needed to give her a flu shot. The syringe really contained a mild sedative. Once the medicine had taken effect, Granny was told about the crash. Wright said that Granny summed up her feelings in one sentence: "If one is gone, I hope they're all gone, because they can't live without each other." Later, she added, "I'd rather have them dead than coming back all mangled."

In Colorado Springs, the airline had called Myra to inform her about the crash. She was alone, except for the poodle, Seric. Fortunately, members of the Broadmoor Skating Club rushed to the house to stay with her. Some of them remember the dog was behaving oddly, howling, whimpering, and pacing in circles, as if he knew the girls were gone. Friends remember that Myra was unusually stoic. For someone so wrapped up in her daughters' every move, she was calm. Rather than allowing others to comfort her as she mourned, she was a gracious host—never cheerful but never dreary, either. She seemed to be presiding over a dull tea party more than a horrible occasion of tragedy. No one is sure who called Otto to report the news, how he reacted, or if he and Myra were civil to each other in their grief. Ironically, the girls' deaths brought Myra her first real taste of financial independence from Otto. She had taken out a large life insurance policy on Steffi and Sherri, which paid $60,000 on their deaths, a large sum in 1961.

In Indianapolis, Rose Anne Ryan woke early, as new mothers often do. Her parents were on their way to Ottawa with two of her daughters when the telephone rang. It was her sister, an Air Canada employee.

"Have you received any calls?" her sister asked. "Have you heard from Mom and Dad?"

The alarming manner in which the questions were posed punched a sickening feeling in Rose Anne's stomach.

Her sister said, "There's been an accident."

"A car accident? Are they hurt?"

"It's worse than that."

"They've been killed? My girls, too?"

A second of silence ensued. Then her sister said, "So you haven't heard from the airlines?"

Almost simultaneously, the doorbell rang. Lulu, the babysitter, was there that morning, and she answered the door to one of Rose Anne's friends, dressed in her pajamas and an overcoat.

Rose Anne's face was now pale. Her sister, the airline worker, had heard about the crash on the morning news and called Sabena to confirm that Danny was on the plane. Rose Anne staggered into the kitchen, where Lulu was on her knees praying. The two boys repeatedly asked what was wrong. Rose Anne hurried to her bedroom, where she dressed for church.

Schoolchildren attending the Mass said prayers for all the families that had lost loved ones. Later that day, the priest came to the house and sat with Rose Anne to pray.

The state police tracked down Rose Anne's parents, and they turned around and headed back to Indianapolis to help their daughter in the height of her grief.

At the same time, in Seattle, Ray Hadley found out his wife and children were dead. He had scheduled his flight to Prague a day later so he could keep his skating studio open one more day. His hushed voice told reporters, "We should have gone together." He had one request: "I just don't want anyone around now. I've asked everyone to stay away."

In Los Angeles, 1976 Olympic silver medalist Diane de Leeuw was only four years old and was watching her morning cartoons when a news bulletin suddenly interrupted. A news anchor spoke through the small black-and-white set and announced, "The entire U.S. figure skating team has perished in a plane crash in Belgium."

Diane's mother, Annie, heard screams from the family room.

"They're all dead, Mommy," Diane shouted. "Everybody's dead!"

Annie ran into the room to investigate the commotion, and saw the end of the news bulletin. She then clutched her sobbing daughter tightly in a failed attempt to console her. Little Diane was already on the ice at her tender age, and the person she looked up to the most was U.S. bronze medalist Rhode Michelson, the gifted jumping bean out of Paramount, California. Now that striking young lady, whose speed and athleticism captured everyone's attention, was dead.

In Rye, New York, Diana LeMaire was only ten years old, and was startled from her sleep by the sound of car doors slamming in her driveway. Her instincts told her something was wrong. As she tumbled out of bed, rubbing her eyes as she walked, she glanced up to see several family friends in the home, some who seemed to have just rolled out of bed themselves. In a day where children were seen rather than heard, Diana was not immediately apprised of the news. She waited patiently until her mother was ready. Clutching her children's hands, Diana's mother, Muriel, sat her children down at the kitchen table.

"We should be thankful that we had a father and we had a brother, even for a short time," she told them. "We should be thankful we ever had them in our lives."

On a Hollywood sound stage, 1960 Olympic skating gold medalist Carol Heiss was beginning a day's work on the set of *Snow White and the Three Stooges* when she was informed about the crash. The vibrant Carol went numb, but bravely continued preparing for her role, as the memories of her young Olympic roommate, Laurence Owen, played back like a movie in her mind. Her compassionate costars gave her a few days off, halting production on what would be her only Hollywood film.

Carol was sought after for comment over and over again. She somberly told reporters after leaving the set, "All our top figure skaters were aboard. I had competed against all of them. This will about do it for our figure skating for some time."

The morning at Winchester Academy got off to its normal start on February 15, 1961, but when the news bulletins reached the principal's office, he knew that he must inform the students. That tranquil morning turned into a daylong remembrance of Laurence Owen, one of the school's star pupils—and America's new skating queen.

Principal W. Howard Niblock announced news of the crash on the public address system, his voice choking on his words.

"If there is one happy note for Laurence in this tragedy," he said, "it was that her death came at her moment of greatest triumph—her victory at the North American Championships."

A moment of silence with a brief prayer followed. Laurence's own words echoed throughout the classrooms that day, as her teachers read her poetry from pieces of notebook paper. But the beauty of her words could not erase an ugly phrase that kept being repeated over and over again: "They're all dead."

Ron Ludington was supposed to be on that plane. He was supposed to be with his students. But he was, instead, broke and living in the YMCA. He did not have his own phone but answered when he heard the hallway phone ringing.

His sister's crackling voice spoke those words: "They're all dead."

Guilt weighed heavily on a former skater in Kansas City. Jane Bucher Jones had first convinced Myra Westerfeld to explore ice skating lessons for her children.

"I read it in a newspaper and I was aghast," she recalled years later. "I was devastated thinking that I had kind of started the ball rolling."

The Western Union service was immediately jammed with condolence messages from skating clubs, dignitaries, and fans around the world. Even in the height of the Cold War, diplomatic conflict was pushed aside, and Soviet President Nikita Kruschev sent a condolence letter.

Kruschev's American counterpart had reason to take the news personally. Thousands of daily newspapers printed President John Kennedy's condolence message:

> "I was distressed and saddened to learn of the airline crash in Brussels this morning. The disaster has brought tragedy to many American families and is a painful loss to the international community of sports as well. Our country has sustained a great loss of talent and grace which has brought pleasure to people all over the world. Mrs. Kennedy and I extend our deepest sympathy to the families and friends of all the passengers and crew who died in the crash."

The Kennedys, of course, were painfully familiar with air disasters. The President's older brother, Joe Jr., died in a plane crash while serving in World War II in 1944. His sister Kathleen died in a plane crash in 1948.

Edward Kennedy was an assistant district attorney in Boston when he learned about the crash. He had just phoned one of his best friends and Harvard roommate, Dudley Richards, the day before the flight to wish him luck.

"It seemed that Dudley was really hitting his stride at the time of the crash," Kennedy recalled. "We always enjoyed his successes skating. We had a good friendship. I still remember his smile and his dedication. After the crash, we were all just shattered. The loss was tremendous."

Edward, who inherited the Kennedy genius of public speaking, would give his most difficult speech to date that year. He would deliver the eulogy at his friend's funeral.

Despite the immense tragedy, Lorraine Hanlon was still required to attend school on February 15. Throughout the day, only one teacher acknowledged the massive emotional burden she was carrying. That teacher said simply, "This must be a difficult day for you."

In Prague, a plane's wheels screeched loudly on a runway. Its passengers were stepping behind the mythical Iron Curtain for the first time, a fact that put them in a rare class in contentious times between world superpowers. When the plane's stairs descended to the frigid tarmac, weary Canadian travelers who were about to represent their country on the world stage of sport walked off. Otto and Maria Jelinek were passengers on the plane. Their hearts beat quickly in both fear and excitement about returning to their country of birth. In the terminal, they looked around and noticed a conspicuous absence.

Maria asked an airport employee,"Where are the Americans?"

With not a hint of emotion, the man simply answered, "They are not coming. They are all dead."

Maria began to sob. Her Canadian teammates initially thought the uniformed airport officer was arresting them because their family had defected.

In Canada, a reporter called the Jelinek home to report that the plane had crashed, and that their children were dead. When Mrs. Jelinek had last spoken to Otto and Maria, they were holding tickets to Sabena Flight 548. Mrs. Jelinek didn't know that the coach had intervened, changing their flights while unknowingly rescuing them from the hands of death.

A steady stream of consolation poured into the house, and two parents were starting to think of burying their children. Then, hours later, the phone rang. Mrs. Jelinek picked up. It was a newspaper reporter who had been at Idlewild Airport and had watched Otto and Maria board a different plane. There were alive. There were loud cries on the line as the emotion brought the parents to their knees in thanks.

More than a week after the crash, Maribel Vinson Owen and her two daughters were brought home and interred at the Mount Auburn Cemetery in Cambridge, Massachusetts. Ron Ludington was among the mourners at their funeral. Maribel was his coach, and a force in his life. After the Owen funerals Ron had an important visit to make. He went to that stately house on High Street, where Granny Vinson now resided, alone. While sitting on the couch visiting with Granny and reminiscing, he suddenly noticed a ghostly piece of memorabilia.

Years later, he recalled,"I was sitting there with her and chatting about the old times, and I looked up at the fireplace mantle and saw the pack of cigarettes that Maribel took away from me two years earlier." In hindsight, he wishes he would have taken the pack as a

Courtesy of Pikes Peak Library Distict

Myra Westerfeld, her brother, and mother leave Steffi and Sherri's memorial service.

memento, but he didn't have the heart to ask Granny.

Newspaper accounts of the crash didn't heal any wounds. The *Los Angeles Times* featured the headline, "Magazine's hex hits again as skater dies." The skater to which the paper referred was Laurence Owen, the *Sports Illustrated* cover girl the day Sabena Flight 548 crashed. The paper noted that in early 1955, American skier Jill Kinmont was paralyzed in a ski accident after appearing on the magazine's cover. In 1958, Irish race car driver Pat O'Connor was on the cover the week of the Indianapolis 500. He died in a fiery pileup on lap one of the race.

As the families mourned, skaters converged on Prague for the World Championship. All the pageantry that seems to accompany

any major sporting event ground to a halt. Maria and Otto, like many other skaters, practiced with empty hearts.

"None of us felt like competing," Maria said.

In the city that had invested hundreds of thousands of dollars in hosting the event, there was suddenly talk of canceling it to show the proper reverence for the lost American team. Bitter Czech officials, suspecting some sort of Western conspiracy, angrily pointed out that several members of the Czech hockey team perished in a plane crash in 1947, but the World Hockey Championships went on as planned in London.

F. Ritter Shumway of the USFSA believed the event should go on as scheduled. He said simply, "The skaters would have wanted it that way."

Everyone gave an opinion, but with the event scheduled for just a week after the crash, there wasn't much time to render a decision. In Davos, Switzerland, the executive committee of the International Skating Union voted to cancel the meet just a day after the crash, "As a sign of mourning over the deaths of our United States comrades."

Shumway, despite his disagreement with the decision, thanked the international skating community for the supreme gesture of sympathy and compassion.

"I know I speak for all members of the USFSA when I say we are deeply moved by this expression of sympathy," he said. "This sincere feeling of fellowship evidenced by such a sacrifice eases the burden that all of us in the United States feel and indicates the high personal regard in which our skaters were held throughout the world."

The World Championships were promised to Prague in 1962.

Maria and Otto went on to perform in the scheduled exhibitions in Europe, but the theme of the performances had been changed to reflect the tragedy. Before each performance, the names of the

American team members were announced with a long spotlight glaring onto a hauntingly empty ice surface.

As the final funerals took place, families of the victims struggled with Sabena Airlines, the company that had been so eager to get the business of the American team. Coaches and chaperones of the victims had been required to pay for themselves. Families were left to tangle with Sabena over refunds for the cost of the plane tickets. Months after the tragedy, family members were still trying to track down personal effects belonging to the victims. In many cases, it was impossible to prove what belonged to whom, so numerous items remained unclaimed at Sabena's New York offices. Families also had to track down numbers from unused traveler's checks. On October 9, 1961, Sabena issued ticket refunds in the amount of $4,687.20.

Many families sought legal counsel in an effort to sue the airline. Under the Warsaw Convention, the airline's liability was capped at $8,300 per person, unless "gross negligence" could be proven. Several families united to sue the airline in U.S. District Court for $11,200,000 in damages. They waited for the final crash report to be released to use as evidence to bolster their case.

In skating circles, Shumway will always be remembered as the grandfatherly central figure of consolation for most of the family members of crash victims. He exchanged dozens of letters with the families of victims. He responded to each letter with the most personal touch possible. He spoke at dozens of memorial services and memorial ice shows.

He saw to it that the families each received a copy of the 16mm Kodak film shot at the National and North American championships. While not every skater was seen on the broadcast, a local television cameraman had filmed some of the excluded performances. Rendering this film even more precious was the fact that another film—this one with all the skaters—had been lost. For years, Howard Craker had recorded the U.S. National Skating

Championships for the association. His film disappeared just days after the tragedy—and was never seen again.

Shumway sent a copy of the CBS tape to Otto Westerfeld. Myra was furious.

On May 30, 1961, Myra pleaded in a letter, "Please, Mr. Shumway, don't sent anything to him. He did not take care of his daughters in the last two years of their young lives, and in death, I do not want him to be informed of anything." It was too late. Ritter had already sent the film to Otto, and fortunately, he never had to deal with this conflict again.

In just under two years, Myra had lost her husband and her daughters. There was one more crushing blow to come. She found out about Sherri's marriage. Sherri's husband, Roberto, told Myra about the eleven-month-long arrangement. Explaining the unusual marriage in a recent interview, Roberto said money prevented them from having a big wedding and from living together. He instead lived with a friend. The couple saw each other every day while Sherri worked in Roberto's jewelry store.

Today he insists Myra did know about the marriage earlier, but friends of the Westerfelds dispute this claim. They say Myra found out about the marriage after the crash and that she only believed the revelation when Roberto showed her the marriage license. It was indeed Sherri's signature on the document.

Myra told friends the marriage was designed to help Roberto gain his U.S. citizenship. She was devastated. Despite this anger, she felt closest to Sherri inside Roberto's store and even took Sherri's job, working there for many years. It appears that Sherri, who Roberto called "flawless," had once again put the needs of others in front of her own happiness.

Two other skating families faced painful conflict after the crash. Several months after the crash, Larry Pierce's parents still had the trophy he and Dee Dee Sherbloom won at Nationals in their last-minute pairing. It had been forgotten in storage. When its whereabouts were revealed, Dee Dee's mother said she wanted the trophy, too. It was agreed that the Pierces and Sherblooms would split the remaining months before the trophy would have to be returned in January of 1962.

When it came time to return the championship trophy, the Pierce family did not immediately respond, greatly upsetting Diane's mother.

Mrs. Sherbloom called the home of the Pierces' daughter, Jan, in California. She left a message with a babysitter and never received a return call. Exasperated, Mrs. Sherbloom wrote a letter to F. Ritter Shumway:

> Mr. Shumway, the day before or the day after Christmas Eve, we received a letter from the Pierce family saying they were here in California. No mention was made about seeing us or visiting Diane's grave, and no mention was made about the trophy. You know, everyone out here knew Diane had no intention of skating last year until Larry, his mother, and father all called several times, and Larry wrote pleading for her to come and skate with Larry, because this was his last year, and if he didn't make it then, it was his last chance. They convinced her against her better judgment, for she thought he should wait until Marilyn was able to skate and also, that she wouldn't be winning for herself, but for Marilyn. After the accident, they (the Pierces) called blaming themselves. I knew they had enough to bear with the loss of their son and didn't want them to be tortured with guilty feelings, so I wrote them a nice letter. I cannot understand people taking the attitude they have taken to myself and my family. They promised to look after her like she was their own daughter.
>
> Apparently they have washed their hands of this whole

> thing and do not want to see us or even visit Diane's grave. Perhaps they feel their son was the only one entitled to the trophy and this is their way of showing it. Now, I don't want to see them or the trophy. I just want to forget before they destroy all of my belief in what's right.

In fairness to the Pierce family, one can certainly understand the complex emotions that must have stirred within their hearts when it came time to return the trophy. The apparent reluctance is something to which any parent can relate. Larry's hopes and dreams, his accomplishments, and his ultimate glory were all symbolized by that stunning and elegant piece of hardware. For the Pierce family, letting go of the trophy was indeed like letting go of Larry all over again. In the final analysis, these two families who never interacted before those fateful weeks of 1961 were now equally covetous of the brightest symbol of their children's ultimate achievements.

Shumway intervened and Mrs. Sherbloom received the trophy on January 30, 1962, just two weeks before she had to give it back to the USFSA for the Nationals. She kept it on display at Diane's skating club, where her younger daughter was also training. Mrs. Sherbloom encouraged Ritter to require the USFSA to insure skaters before taking plane trips. Only a handful of the skaters did not have life insurance when they died. Dee Dee was one of them. Her sister was permitted to train for free until the October following the crash.

While friends and family members tried to heal, politicians were busy with their own agendas regarding the crash. A little more than a month after the crash, U.S. Congressman Walter Rogers of Texas sent a letter to Shumway inquiring about the choice of Sabena Airlines. He was on the Interstate and Foreign Commerce Committee and was looking into reasons international air carriers were frequently chosen over domestic carriers.

"This was indeed a great tragedy and I have delayed getting in touch with you until some of the resulting grief and sorrow had subsided," he wrote in the letter.

Shumway explained some of the reasons for the selection of Sabena, which included, among other things, a fear of Cold War sabotage on non-American planes, especially in light of a recent Russian air disaster.

Shumway quipped in a return letter, "Their experience with the American-made Boeing 707 was no better."

A little more than two years after the crash of Sabena Flight 548, the Belgian government released the official crash report. Families eagerly awaited the news, in their quest to find out what happened in those final moments of their loved ones' lives.

In the report, the flight was described as "normal in every respect," until its approach to runway twenty at Brussels International Airport. This is the report summary, taken from the point when the pilot was given clearance to land.

> Instead of landing, the pilot, near the runway threshold, increases power and retracts the undercarriage. The aircraft gains some height and executes several circles in a left turn. During these evolutions the bank angle—while however decreasing several times for short periods—increases more and more until finally the aircraft crashes and fire breaks out upon impact. The eleven crewmembers and sixty-one passengers are fatally injured. The aircraft is completely destroyed. One person on the ground is killed; another severely injured.

One of the leading hypotheses in the transcript of the crash report is a possible defect in the plane's spoilers. However, it was impossible for the commission to determine if there was a spoiler defect before takeoff, or if the damage resulted from the crash itself. Despite a thorough review of the flight data and voice transmissions, a conclusion was never reached as to a specific cause.

> Having done all possible reasonable investigations, the Commission concludes that the cause of the accident must be looked for in the physical failure of the flying controls. However, while it was possible to advance certain hypotheses relative to these possible causes, it must remark that they generate certain objections and can therefore not be considered as entirely satisfactory. Only the physical failure of two systems can lead to a complete explanation, but leaves the door open to an arbitrary choice because there is not sufficient evidence to corroborate it.

The United States Federal Aviation Administration also reviewed data from the plane crash, and believed the plane's stabilizer malfunctioned. The Belgian commission recommended several modifications to Boeing, which included changes to the spoilers, the control wheel stabilizer, the inboard aileron, the hydraulic system valves, and the rudder control spring cables. The commission further recommended the installation of a supplementary brake for the stabilizer actuator. The commission also asked Boeing to introduce a spoiler position indicator that would bring any abnormalities to the crew's attention. In addition to carrying out those recommendations, Boeing added a vertical stabilizer fin under the tail of its 707 model.

While the crash report did very little to prove any gross negligence on the part of Sabena, the airline chose to settle out of court with the victims' families in 1965. The lawsuit records were sealed for perpetuity.

When Sabena Flight 548 crashed, it did more than shatter

unrealized dreams. It changed the flight habits of U.S. figure skating delegations. Since the crash of Sabena Flight 548, an entire U.S. figure skating team has never flown overseas on the same plane.

Other sports teams, however, continue the practice of keeping teams together. The crash of Sabena Flight 548 was not the first time that this had resulted in tragedy, nor would it be the last. Perhaps some of those on Sabena Flight 548 had even heard of the earlier crashes, and carried dim, fearful recollections with them in the back of their minds as they boarded their own flight. In May of 1949, eighteen members of the powerful Torino, Italy, soccer team, along with six trainers, died when their plane crashed in a thunderstorm. In February of 1958, eight members of the Manchester United soccer team were among twenty-three people (out of forty-four aboard) who were killed when a British European Airways Airspeed Ambassador airliner crashed. In July of 1960, eight members of the Danish soccer team died in a plane crash. In October of 1960, sixteen members of the California Poly San Luis Obispo football team were killed when their chartered plane crashed shortly after taking off from the Toledo, Ohio, airport.

In 1970, one of two chartered planes carrying the Wichita State University football team crashed, killing thirty-one of the forty people on board. In November of 1970, seventy-five people, including forty-three members of the Marshall University football team, were killed when a Southern Airways DC-9 crashed in the mountains of West Virginia. In 1972, a plane carrying members of Uruguay's soccer team crashed in the Chilean Andes. There were thirty-two survivors out of the forty-five people on board. When help did not arrive immediately, the desperate and starving survivors cannibalized some of those killed. When help came seventy-two days later, only sixteen survivors remained. The crash inspired the book and movie *Alive*.

In December of 1977, the University of Evansville basketball team was killed when a National Jet Services DC-3 crashed during takeoff from Evansville, Indiana. Twenty-nine players, coaches, and officials and crewmembers were killed. In 1980, twenty-two members of the U.S. Olympic boxing team, along with sixty-four others, were killed while attempting to land in Poland.

What sets the crash of Sabena Flight 548 apart was that not only did eighteen star athletes die, but the entire sport of figure skating was wounded—some feared, beyond repair. Almost all of the nation's top coaches were killed. The athletes killed were considered the definitive choices for the 1964 Olympic team. The recovery process was expected to be arduous. But if the skating program could show the resilience the American skaters had shown during their short lives, there was hope.

Chapter Twelve

Obliterated.

The word was used countless times in headlines, used to describe the state of American figure skating, and any hopes for continued dominance in world and Olympic competition. Dick Button had won two Olympic gold medals in a row, followed by Hayes Alan and David Jenkins. Tenley Albright and Carol Heiss each won a gold in the years prior to the crash. American pairs teams were regulars on the podium, too, and it seemed it wouldn't take long for an American pair to climb all the way to the gold medal position.

But that word—obliterated—kept appearing, wounding anew the people who cared deeply about a sport already so intensely wrapped in emotion. The word rang out like a death knell, coming to be synonymous with the shattered hopes and dreams of those skaters who died, and the unlikely prospects that any of the remaining skaters could mount a legitimate challenge to the more established world competitors.

At best, the American skating team was a year behind. Realistically, the program would take several years to rebuild. It was a rare, perhaps even unprecedented, time in the history of American athletics, when an entire sport had to reinvent itself—its stars and its leading coaches. Laurence and Steffi were considered contenders for a 1964 Olympic medal. Laurence, quite possibly, could have won the gold, although Sjouhke Dijkstra of Holland was the reigning Olympic silver medalist and a better bet for the top spot. If Rhode could have made strides in her school figures and her artistry, she could have been a dark horse in the medal hunt. It was even more likely that Laurence, Steffi, and Rhode would reach the apex of their careers at the 1968 Winter Olympics. They would have been twenty-four. As Dudley Richards proved by winning his first national title in 1961 at age twenty-nine, a skater could compete well into his or her twenties.

Bradley Lord, the quiet men's champion with his eyes sharply focused on a career, likely would have retired after the 1964 Olympics, leaving energetic and exuberant Gregory Kelley to carry on through 1968. In the pairs event, Mara and Dud were performing maneuvers as difficult as some of the most famous pairs teams in the world, and could have won medals, too, although they may not have been as strong as some of the dominant European teams. It is impossible to accurately conclude what glory they would have known, what dreams they would have fulfilled, and what family legacies they would have sealed.

The Figure Skating Club of Boston rink, a vibrant, intense breeding ground for champions, was eerily quiet after the crash. A wreath was hung in remembrance of the skaters, but it offered no peace or cheer to the young novice- and junior-level skaters left behind. The ice was crystal clear, with not a single trace of figure eights or serpentine patterns, not a single jagged hole from a fast-moving toe pick gnashing into the ice. A solemn silence pervaded the rink.

But there was no time to mourn. There was no time to remember or cry for friends who were so respected and admired. The next

Nationals competition would take place in eleven months, and from that event the 1962 Worlds team would be chosen. The 1964 Olympic hopes would be born anew. And at the 1962 Nationals, the spirits of Laurence, Steffi, and all the other young dreamers would preside.

In the 1961 Nationals, Laurence, Steffi, Mara, Dud, Bradley, Gregory, and Larry Pierce were all familiar names—not famous, but familiar. In 1962, a crop of no-name skaters was expected to launch U.S. skating into prominence again. It was like starting from scratch, with crucial ingredients missing from the recipe for Olympic glory.

And so the first skaters took their timid glides onto the untouched ice surface in Boston. The same ritual played out at the Broadmoor Ice Palace in Colorado Springs, where there was another conspicuous absence. Edi Scholdan, the reliable rock of skating in the Western United States, was dead. He was not there to hold court over the laughter of his pupils, who loved his lampoons of newspaper headlines. The remaining skaters and coaches couldn't help but feel guilty, but deep in their hearts, they knew Edi would want them to carry on for the love of skating, and for the hope of rising to podiums in the future.

F. Ritter Shumway called to order several meetings to discuss rebuilding the United States team. The talents of novice- and junior-level skaters were analyzed, picked apart, and studied. The concerns about what they needed to learn to compete internationally were surpassed only by the question of *who* was going to teach them.

British-born John Nicks, a 1953 world champion in pairs, was living with his sister in Vancouver, Canada. He had been trying without success to land a coaching job at skating clubs in North America.

"I tried for three months to get a teaching job in Canada," he recalled. "Nobody would hire me there. I finally woke up one morning and heard about the terrible air crash, and about four or six weeks later, I wrote to the secretary of the USFSA asking if he could recommend me to any club or ice rink. I think he looked around, and I got three job offers. One was from Cleveland, and one was from Paramount in Long Beach, California."

John, thinking of the nice weather, chose Paramount, the home of the Arctic Blades Figure Skating Club. "I was replacing Bill Kipp, who was killed in the crash. It was a little difficult to start with, because the local skaters and coaches were feeling their loss, and I was feeling their loss at the same time. After I was there for a while, things became comfortable."

Kipp, called "Billy," was a native of Allentown, Pennsylvania, and had moved to Paramount to coach. He was an expert in dance and singles skating and was coaching Rhode Michelson and the dance team of Dona Lee Carrier and Roger Campbell in 1961. He was outspoken about his view that ice dancing should be included in the Olympics.

"The dance in figure skating is not considered an Olympic sport, and I don't think that is correct or fair," he told a reporter for the *Allentown Morning Call* in an interview before boarding the plane. His dream would be realized in 1976, when the ice dance made its debut at the Innsbruck, Austria, Winter Olympics.

At the Broadmoor Ice Skating Club, another charismatic European, Carlo Fassi, would be hired to replace Edi Scholdan. John Nicks remembers that both he and Carlo were deeply stricken by the irony of their success.

"We talked a lot about the irony of the event that brought us here, that it was so tragically sad, but afforded a great opportunity for us. The whole issue of the crash, and the sadness involved, was very difficult to come to terms with. I was amazed when I got to California about the ambition of the young people in figure skating, and the intensity with which they trained, that the families have in this endeavor. I think it is responsible for the success America has had over the last sixty years."

Nicks and Fassi were crucial in rebuilding the U.S. skating program, as was Frank Carroll, one of Maribel Vinson Owen's former students. He has coached champions Linda Fratianne, Michelle Kwan, Timothy Goebel, and most recently, Evan Lysacek. Among John Nicks's many successes are Ken Shelley and JoJo Starbuck, Tai Babilonia and Randy Gardner, Christopher Bowman, and most recently, Sasha Cohen.

Ron Ludington, now called "Luddy" by his students, should have been on Sabena Flight 548 with his dancers Robert and Patricia Dineen. Already broke and in the middle of a divorce, he had hardly anyone to coach after the crash. Ironically, his first full-time job offer came just a few months later at the Winter Club in Indianapolis, where his friend Daniel Ryan had been the lead pro before his death. He has since coached numerous champions, such as Olympic silver medalists Caitlin and Peter Curruthers, and 1988 Olympians Nathalie and Wayne Seybold.

With coaches in place, the process of building a championship team remained the primary goal. The USFSA was worried that the lack of experience of the younger skaters would show an embarrassing lack of depth in the skating program at the 1962 Worlds. To improve medal hopes, 1960 Olympic bronze medalist Barbara Roles was coaxed out of retirement, though she now was married and had a seven-month-old child. The team needed to have at least one skater finish in the top five at Worlds to ensure that it could send three skaters in each event in 1963. This rule of international competition loomed over the event.

The championship trophies had at last been returned to the United States Figure Skating Association. The last names etched into their silver were the names of the dead. Fans of the sport expected the

Bob Gomel/Time & Life Pictures/Getty Images

Tina Noyes made the 1964 Olympic team at age fifteen. She was one of the young novice skaters who helped replenish U.S. Olympic hopes after the crash.

1962 Nationals to be full of duress and emotional discord, but the event turned out to be a fine success. It was held in Boston—which lost six skaters, more than any other club, in the crash. The youngsters asked to fill those shoes faced a lot of stress and demands.

Tina Noyes, only thirteen, was one of the up-and-comers. On the fortieth anniversary of the crash, she recalled to the *Boston Globe*, "There were a lot of high expectations, a tremendous amount of pressure."

Despite the pressure, the competitors prepared with energy and enthusiasm. The crash did not in any way make the 1962 Nationals a depressing event. In fact, holding the competition with the usual regalia seemed the most fitting and proper way to honor the skaters and coaches who had died.

While the tragedy wasn't mentioned much, there were a

Ralph Crane/Time & Life Pictures/Getty Images

The 1960 U.S. Olympians Carol Heiss (third from right) and Barbara Roles (second from left) had retired prior to 1961. Barbara Roles returned to help the U.S. team recover in 1962.

few reminders here and there. The official program for the event read, "A unique set of circumstances finds us without defending champions this year." Small pictures of the 1961 champions were placed in the program.

Barbara Roles, who brought her baby to the competition, was ready to take the ice for her compulsory figures when she discovered she was within minutes of being disqualified. The start time for the figures had been changed, but nobody had called Barbara to tell her.

At twenty, Barbara was between four and eight years older than the other competitors she faced but still was not considered too old to skate. Tina Noyes also recalled to the *Boston Globe* in 2001 that, "Her coming back was really huge. I remember when she came into the Skating Club to practice. Everything just stopped. It was almost like looking at a ghost."

With the exception of Barbara, the ladies event resembled more of a girls event; the beautiful, healthy curves of the 1961 ladies were replaced with scrawny girls forced into an awkward-looking grownup role.

The next day in the free skate, Barbara won her first U.S. National title. Lorraine Hanlon, who looked up to Laurence in life, won a silver medal in the senior ladies event, while Victoria Fisher, who was edged by Rhode Michelson for a medal in 1961, won a bronze.

In the men's event, the podium was composed of mere boys. Monty Hoyt took the gold, followed by the youngster Scott Ethan Allen, with the bronze medal won by David Edwards. Scott Allen was only twelve years old and not even a hundred pounds. Not to diminish the accomplishment of these three young men, but it is worth mentioning that only four men competed.

In the pairs event, Pieter Kollen and Dorothyann Nelson took home the gold, followed by silver medal winners Judianne and Jerry Fotheringill. The 1961 junior champions Vivian and Ronald Joseph won the bronze.

In dance, Yvonne Littlefield (once a partner of Roger Campbell) and Peter Betts won gold, followed by Dorothyann Nelson and Pieter Kollen, and Lorna Dyer and King Cole.

Each champion of the 1962 Nationals had won for the first time. None would ever win at Nationals again.

The youthful and inexperienced brigade would travel to Prague for the World Championships. This time, and every time since the crash of Sabena Flight 548, the team members would be booked on separate planes.

Canadians Otto and Maria Jelinek were again faced with the frightening prospect of competing in their home country. The German Gestapo had tormented their prominent family during the World War II occupation, and the Czech communist government later confiscated their family home. Memories of their country

Art Shay/Time & Life Pictures/Getty Images

Scott Ethan Allen won an Olympic bronze medal in 1964 at age fourteen.

obviously were not always happy ones. They would have heavy hearts too, thinking of Mara and Dud, and the moment they learned of their deaths. Flying to Prague gave everyone an uneasy feeling.

In a strange twist, *ABC's Wide World of Sports* broadcast the World Figure Skating Championships for the first time and has done so ever since. One can only imagine the global fame the 1961 team would have achieved, and how the European viewers would have marveled at Laurence's almost Parisian flair, and how Maribel would relish every moment.

At the competition, the Americans were not an embarrassment; they were an inspiration. Barbara Roles hardly had time to train and still placed fifth. Lorraine Hanlon placed tenth. Victoria Fisher came in sixteenth. However, Wendy Griner, the Canadian girl Laurence had beaten in two of their three meetings, won a silver medal behind Sjouhke Dijkstra of Holland. Laurence, it appeared, would have won some kind of medal if fate had not intervened.

Monty Hoyt of the U.S. placed sixth for the men, and Scott Allen was eighth. In the dance event, Pieter Kollen and Dorothyann Nelson finished seventh, with Yvonne Littlefield and Peter Betts in eighth.

While Don Jackson, the men's gold medal winner, had dazzled the world by landing the first-ever triple Lutz in competition, the real stars of the event were Otto and Maria. Their program was powerful, perfect, and emotional. The Czech crowd applauded in a way that said, "Welcome home." Following the event, they were invited to the Austrian embassy for dinner. It just so happened the embassy was Otto and Maria's childhood home—the home that had been taken away from them.

The best American finish in pairs was Pieter Kollen and Dorothyann Nelson, who finished eighth—an astounding success considering they competed in both the dance and pairs, a feat that is very rare in world competitive circles today.

The first steps in the painful path of rebuilding had been taken. All eyes were fixed on the 1964 Olympics. Barbara Roles decided to retire again, and so Lorraine Hanlon seemed to offer the best hope for a medal, but she retired after winning Nationals in 1963. She had suffered through a broken foot and then traveled to Switzerland to train and study before she finally decided to discover life after skating.

As the 1964 Nationals approached the field still looked thin, and the winners would represent the United States at the Innsbruck, Austria, Olympics. Then, out of the shadows leapt a wondrous young beauty, an elegant portrait of loveliness, who brought a special, lyrical quality to her skating. Peggy Fleming burst onto the scene, winning her first national championship at age fifteen. The title of national champion would belong to her for five more years, which in the skating world is considered a dynasty.

At the Olympics, Peggy placed sixth. The two other American youngsters, Tina Noyes and Christine Haigler, placed seventh and eighth, respectively. The American hero of the Games was Scott Ethan Allen, who won a surprise bronze medal with the performance of a lifetime. He was the youngest American men's national champion in history, winning at age fourteen. He proudly stood on the Olympic podium and watched the American flag rise in his honor. In the pairs event, a strange development occurred. Vivian and Ronald Joseph officially finished fourth but were given a set of bronze medals when it was revealed the silver medalists from Germany had signed a professional contract before the Games. The Germans' silver medals were never returned, and they were never officially removed from the record books as silver medalists.

With those performances, the U.S. skating program had defied predictions and recovered faster than anyone would have imagined. Though the program had not returned to its era of dominance, it had made a strong showing and seemed headed in a positive direction.

Following the 1964 Olympics, Peggy Fleming moved from California to Colorado Springs to train with Carlo Fassi. Her school figures needed improvement before she could be a strong competitor on the international scene. In 1965, she won her first medal at the World Championships—a bronze. In 1966 and 1967, she won the gold. As a reigning world champion, she was the overwhelming favorite heading into the 1968 Olympics in Grenoble, France.

Peggy took to the ice wearing a light-green, hand-sewn dress and sporting a classic "up" hairdo. She had amassed such a large lead during the compulsory figures that only calamity could prevent her from bringing the gold medal home to the United States.

Peggy's performance was hypnotic in its simplicity and cleanness. She had singled a planned double Axel and double-footed her double Lutz, but the quality of her skating cast a spell on television viewers, who were seeing figure skating in color for the first time. Following her win, she appeared on the cover of *Life* magazine. Not long after that, she signed a half-million-dollar deal with the Ice Follies—the biggest payout to a skater since Sonja Henie's movie studio contract.

Sports Illustrated wrote of Peggy in 1994, "She launched figure skating's modern era. Pretty and balletic, elegant and stylish, Fleming took a staid sport that was shackled by its inscrutable compulsory figures and arcane scoring system and, with television as her ally, made it marvelously glamorous. Ever since, certainly to North Americans, figure skating has been the marquee sport of the Winter Games and increasingly a staple of prime-time television." That year, the magazine named Fleming one of the forty individuals who most significantly impacted sports in the previous forty years. Her gold medal was an achievement shared by the entire American skating program, still wondering out loud "what could have been" for the skaters who had died only seven years earlier. The 1968 Grenoble Olympics signaled that the recovery was now complete. Who knows how the script of Peggy Fleming's life would have changed had the crash of Sabena Flight 548 not occurred?

In her book, *The Long Program, Skating Toward Life's Victories*, she said, "If things had developed according to script, I would have stayed with Bill for a number of years and taken my place alongside his pupils, who were among the top U.S. hopefuls.

"But then there was the crash. A missing generation of skaters

Hulton Archive/Getty Images

Peggy Fleming's victory at the 1968 Winter Olympics demonstrated the U.S. skating program had fully rebounded from the 1961 crash.

left a big empty space on the ice for the younger athletes, and I was among them."

Granny Vinson, the sole survivor in the Vinson Owen legacy, lived just long enough to see Peggy Fleming's victory at the 1968 Olympics. Following the crash, she remained close to the skaters of the Figure Skating Club of Boston, coming to watch practices and cheer for everyone when she could. She died less than a year after Peggy's victory, very likely wondering how the Olympic podium—and her own family legacy—may have looked if not for the cruel circumstances of 1961.

Afterword

Out of the ashes of tragedy rose profound generosity.

Following the crash of Sabena Flight 548, thousands of condolence messages poured into the Boston headquarters of the United States Figure Skating Association. They were written in dozens of languages, their ink sometimes smeared by teardrops. The U.S. skating program lay mortally wounded, and Americans grieved by opening their wallets. The flow of green first came during tribute performances to the lost team.

The hard-hit Boston skating community came together for memorial shows on March 28 and 29, 1961. Broadcast on local television, the official program included biographies of the Boston skaters, coaches, and officials who died. The performers included Dick Button, David Jenkins of the U.S., Donald Jackson of Canada, and the pairs team of Barbara Wagner and Robert Paul, also of Canada. Proceeds from the show were directed into a new memorial fund.

Edward Kennedy was there, too, and read a special message written by his brother, President John F. Kennedy. Just a few days after the performance, the United States Figure Skating Association suffered another major blow. Association Secretary Harold G. Storke died suddenly—leaving yet another pair of shoes to be filled.

On May 6, 1961, New York City hosted a packed tribute performance. F. Ritter Shumway announced to the crowd that in the weeks after the tragedy $50,000 had been directed into the new fund. Much of that money was unsolicited. Over the next few years, the USFSA would meet, form committees, and ultimately decide how to appropriate money from the Memorial Fund.

There was general agreement that the money should be used in a productive and lasting way, rather than on a memorial statue or something similar. In the beginning, monies were used to conduct skating clinics and seminars. The fund soon developed into a means to help gifted skaters with the financial strains of the sport. Competitive skaters who show promise as world competitors, and fit the appropriate financial profile, are now assisted with payments for coaching, ice time, equipment, choreography and dance classes, off-ice training, costumes, physical therapy, and medical expenses.

President John F. Kennedy praised the formation of the fund.

"The losses which were sustained in the Brussels tragedy are irreparable. However, you are assuring a new surge of interest in figure skating, and the Memorial Fund gives promise that there will be a fresh release of talent and creativity in the years ahead."

Shumway expressed his vision for the Memorial Fund in his opening remarks at the first-ever Memorial Fund Benefit Performance of the Ice Capades on September 18, 1961.

> "It is often in times of tragedy that the finest and most unselfish aspects of human character become evident. The loss of our 1961 World Figure Skating Team, officials, relatives and friends in the airplane tragedy in Belgium was no exception. It has been one of the most moving experiences of my life to receive, on behalf of the United States Figure Skating Association, expressions of sympathy from all over the world, and to witness the deep and sincere feelings of mutual loss that have been exhibited by skaters of all countries, professional and amateur alike. We will take our Memorial Fund a giant skating stroke forward toward our goal of perpetuating the memory of our gallant 1961 World Team skaters, not so much by statuary and plaques, as by giving us the means to assist talented young skaters, many of them yet 'undiscovered,' to get started, to develop and advance, and eventually to represent our

> country in future years, and to be ranked at the top of the world in the art of figure skating."

Peggy Fleming said of the fund, "I'm from a family of four girls; my dad was a newspaper pressman and didn't make much money at all. My mom just took care of us, so we were really strapped financially for me to compete in skating. The fund was just starting then, but it helped—like buying me a pair of skates. That was huge help back then."

Mark Mitchell, the 1993 U.S. men's silver medalist, and two-time World Team competitor, understands the importance of the Memorial Fund. He knows that in skating, the better you get, the more expensive the sport becomes.

> "You have coaching fees, which can run anywhere form $60-$120 an hour, and most kids get a minimum of one lesson every day. You have to buy the ice time, which can be very expensive. Depending on where you live, it can be $10-$15 an hour, and most kids skate for three hours, five days a week at least. And then there are the skates, which run between $800 and $1,000 a pair, and most kids go through two pairs a year. Add in competition expenses—hotels, coach's travel, coach's fees. It adds up, it really does."

Mitchell is now a successful coach at the Skating Club of Boston. Some of Mitchell's pupils are benefiting from the Memorial Fund.

"I think the USFSA does a good job of keeping the memory and spirit of the 1961 team alive through the Fund," he says.

Scott Hamilton's parents were schoolteachers during his rise in the competitive ranks. The Memorial Fund helped ease some of his family's financial strain.

Dan Hollander, a two-time U.S. senior men's bronze medalist and well-loved member of the Champions on Ice Tour, was asked to serve on the Memorial Fund athlete's committee. He received a small stipend from the fund.

Hollander feels that most skaters probably don't know about its tragic origins. "Unfortunately, like most things, many people don't know how it (the Fund) came about. But when the money comes to them, then I think they understand."

Another portion of the Memorial Fund goes into the USFSA academic scholarship program, which assists current and former competitive skaters with funds for enrollment in accredited academic institutions. The money helps with books and supplies. The structure of the Memorial Fund encourages skaters to develop not only as athletes, but as contributors to all facets of society.

Tania Kwiatkowski, the only child of a heavy-equipment operator and a housewife, had golden dreams, too. Tania won a few bronze medals at the United States National Championships, before winning a silver medal in 1996. She knows the incomplete journey of the 1961 team is what helped her in her own journey to the podium, and she doesn't take it for granted.

"It was such a terrible fate for other people, but if the crash had not happened, things would have been a lot harder," she says. "The fund helped my family, and it helped forward my skating."

The Memorial Fund is one the most prominent and substantial legacies of the 1961 team. Bit by bit, society has moved on, leaving behind memories of the victims. They mostly are names in record books; their photos, in black and white, seem of an era long past. The grief-filled letters written by family members to the USFSA gather dust in file folders and boxes with no particular fashion of organization.

Even the venue where their stardom was launched has fallen to the bulldozer. By 1995, the grand old lady of skating rinks was looking decrepit—and, some argued, was becoming downright dangerous. The old rink that hosted some of the world's most famous skaters during their rise to the top was wobbling on her

Photo courtesy of Dixie Wilson

A skate-shaped bench commemorating the Broadmoor skaters who died in 1961 sits outside the hotel.

last legs. The smell of fresh paint and wood that wafted in the air as competitors arrived for the 1961 Nationals had long since faded. The Broadmoor World Arena (formerly called the Ice Palace) stood in the shadow of the luxurious Broadmoor Hotel, a hotel that desperately needed to expand. To pave the way for a new west wing of the hotel, board members decided the rink must go. Hotel owners decided not to rebuild another rink on the hotel property.

The Broadmoor World Arena was rebuilt across town, as a new, state-of-the-art facility. The U.S. Figure Skating Association, which had moved its headquarters from Boston to Colorado Springs on the urging of Broadmoor President Thayer Tutt, was dismayed by the decision not to rebuild in that sentimental location.

There is, however, one remnant of those cherished, but tragic times. Close to the area where the arena once stood, in the exact spot where Edi Scholdan would read his parody of newspaper columns to his laughing pupils, a granite bench shaped as a skate blade stands like a grave marker, with the names of the Broadmoor skaters and coaches who perished etched into its marble.

One lonely woman never visited that bench. She never went to memorial performances. And she never opened up the package containing film canisters of the 1961 Nationals broadcast. She just couldn't bear it.

Myra Westerfeld was a broken lady after 1961. Her beautiful daughters were killed in the crash. Dreams of athletic stardom were shattered. The road to those dreams claimed her marriage, and ultimately, brought death to her most cherished reasons for living. Her strongest living connection to Steffi and Sherri was Seric, the poodle. Outwardly, Myra appeared strong, even displaying her amazing sense of humor to young nieces and nephews. But despite her stoic nature, friends knew her soul was eternally grieving.

A few years after the crash, Seric passed away. Diane Yeomans Robins, a cousin of the Westerfelds, remembers that the dog's death was the first twig in this mighty tree of a woman to snap. "It was her last true link to the girls." Diane said a caretaker at Evergreen Cemetery in Colorado Springs broke the rules and buried the dog near Sherri and Steffi.

Myra died in 1984, five years after Otto Westerfeld died. She was buried next to her daughters and Seric. Only simple gravestones mark the spot where the family was laid to rest. The stones contain no mention of their glories in life. While cleaning out Myra's Colorado house, family members found the canisters of film recorded at the 1961 Nationals. They had collected dust for more than twenty-three years. The family took the film to Kansas City, where the ghostly images of Steffi spinning gracefully on the ice brought a sad hush to all who watched. The family grieved not only for the sisters who died, but for their mother who was too shattered to even watch her beautiful champion daughter after she was gone.

Another mother, Mrs. Lloyd Carrier of Los Angeles, watched the film whenever her cruel insomnia struck. For years after 1961, she routinely awoke at 3 a.m., the moment she found out about the crash. The projector flickered as moving pictures of Dona Lee Carrier and Roger Campbell somehow seemed to bring them back to life, even for just a few moments.

The Hadley Skating Studio, once filled with the scratches of ambitious blades carving out dreams of championships to come, closed just a few years after the crash. The studio's star pupils, Ila Ray and Ray Hadley, died along with their stepmother and coach. Their father was the last one standing in the Hadley brood—but he was barely standing. He continued to take students at the studio until it closed, but he had lost his heart, his soul, and according to friends who knew him, his will to live. Ray Hadley died a few years after the crash, barely over forty, a tattered shadow of himself. His friends say he died of a broken heart.

Five Indianapolis children lost their father on that cold February day in 1961. Rose Anne Wager, the widow of coach Daniel Ryan, moved her children to Lake Placid, New York, to coach year round, and to be closer to her family in Ottawa, Canada. Rose Anne remarried a decade after the Sabena tragedy.

One of the most sympathetic figures from the entire tragedy is Robert Dineen Jr. He was only eight months old when his parents, Robert and Patricia Dineen, died in that Belgian field. Robert's uncle adopted him. He was in the audience when a large crowd gathered in New York City on October 5, 2001, to remember his parents and other victims on the fortieth anniversary of the crash. The event was televised on ABC, but much of the world's focus had turned to a new tragedy, the September 11 terrorist attacks on the United States.

Scott Hamilton said to the crowd, "In 1961, the U.S. figure skating team got hit hard. In 2001, New York and the United States got hit hard."

The memorial extravaganza turned into a double remembrance—for the victims of September 11, and the victims of Sabena Flight 548. A video presentation showed images of a torn and tattered plane lying crippled in a Belgian field, a scene that was perhaps too powerful considering the fact that planes were used as terrorist weapons less than a month before the event. Some of the skaters' families objected to showing the wreckage of the plane.

For Diana LeMaire Squibb, seeing the images of the airplane flashed on the big screen was particularly painful. "I just thought it was in poor taste," she said. "My daddy and big brother were in that plane."

Some of the world's greatest skaters took to the ice in tribute, among them Michelle Kwan. When Kwan won her ninth U.S. figure skating title in 2005, she told reporters, "There's a cosmic connection between me and Maribel. She taught Frank Carroll and Frank coached me for ten years. To be with her [in the record books] is something else." The evening of the tribute performance, Kwan used some of the choreography from Maribel's programs.

Also paying homage to the skating style of the past was Sarah Hughes, who began her program with school figures. Diane Yeomens Robins, Steffi and Sherri's cousin, was particularly moved by Hughes's performance.

"I think it's because Sarah reminds me of Steffi," Diane

explained, adding, "her kindness, genuineness, and there being nothing fake about her." Diane had tickets for the performance, but couldn't bring herself to board a plane so soon after September 11. She watched it on television instead.

The show reportedly brought in six figures for the Memorial Fund, even in a time when most charitable donations were going to the September 11 victims. During the same week, the Belgian government held a memorial at the crash site in Berg-Kampenhout. Family members, crash witnesses, and Sabena officials gathered around a statue dedicated to the memory of the crash victims. Not far away from the memorial site, a new housing addition yielded some painfully preserved mementos of the crash. Hilde and Kristiaan Buys had just moved into their new, white brick home, when they discovered seared seat buckles, steel dinner knives, and random pieces of the charred plane. They decided to keep the pieces in a bucket in their garage, in the chance someone may someday want them.

Another haunting remembrance of the team came to light in 2001. While cataloguing boxes once stored in the Broadmoor Hotel vault, a staff member saw a glistening little pin. The pin read, "Praha, 22-26 Unora, 1961." In English, "Prague, 22-26, February, 1961." U.S. team members wore these commemorative championship pins during the plane ride to Brussels. Officials and judges who had already received their pins were asked to return them out of respect for the team, but not everyone returned them. This pin is believed to have belonged to Broadmoor president Thayer Tutt, who died in 1989. Today, fewer than six of the pins are in existence, most held by private collectors, including the author, who found one at auction. It may have been owned originally by a Czech skating official. The USFSA Hall of Fame and Museum has one as well.

Sabena, the once-mighty airline owned by the Belgian

Photo courtesy of Nikki Nichols

Ron Ludington coaches pupil Kaela Pflumm at the Indy Challenge event in the summer of 2005. Ludington helped rebuild the U.S. skating program.

government, wouldn't last until the next anniversary of the crash. After it was partially sold to SwissAir, both companies went bankrupt. During Sabena's final years of debt-laden operation, travelers had nicknamed the faltering corporate giant "Such A Bad Experience Never Again."

The airline collapsed in November 2001, just two months after the terrorist attacks on the United States. Thousands of passengers were left stranded at airports, and tension was so high that extra police were brought in to keep passengers calm. Even without the terrorist attacks, the airline was likely to fold. Attempts to revive Sabena have failed.

Since the crash, many of the victims have had skating trophies named in their honor. There have been numerous scholarships and awards named after those lost. Many clubs started funds of their own to honor their members who died. In Winchester, Massachusetts, an elementary school was named after Maribel Vinson Owen.

Maribel's biggest rival in life, Sonja Henie, it turned out, also lost her life on a plane. Sonja succumbed to leukemia aboard a flight taking her back to Norway with her husband, where they were to donate some of her artwork and skating memorabilia to a museum. She died only eight years after Maribel.

Boston itself never regained the competitive clout it once had on the skating scene. The majority of ladies singles champions had hailed from Boston in the first half of the twentieth century, but today that is far from the case. Today's shining ladies stars—Michelle Kwan and Sasha Cohen—hail from California. Many of the modern era's men's stars come from dominant skating programs in Michigan. Delaware and Connecticut are the hotbeds of pairs skating and ice dancing.

With each passing year, the memories of the skaters, coaches, officials, and chaperones who died fade even more. Their legacy, however, will never be lost. Tenley Albright, a true legend and ambassador of ice skating, felt Laurence Owen had a real shot at winning a medal, potentially gold, at the 1961 World Championships.

"It was Laurence's year," Albright says. "They were all at a wonderful place in their lives, at a peak."

The officials on the plane—Harold Hartshorne, Deane McMinn, and Walter Powell, were true trailblazers in the sport. Many of the rules and guidelines they created are still in use today. Despite the devastating losses of such skating pioneers, the crash brought about a new awakening for the U.S. skating program.

Ron Ludington believes it brought new prominence to the sport. "The sport kept getting more popular," he says. "The plane crash had a tendency to make more people interested in the sport."

Now, every state in the union has at least one figure skating club.

Ron, ironically, has only missed one World Championship in the last fifty years—and that was 1961.

It is impossible to speculate what these young skaters would have accomplished, and how the record books would look different had they lived. In their short lives, the skaters were already top citizens. Most of them had interests and talents beyond skating. They were coin collectors, pianists, dancers, swimmers, skiers, singers, poets and members of the Harvard elite. They possessed limitless and unrealized potential. Skating historian Ben Wright sums it rather eloquently.

"When people die so young, they remain forever young."

And in the eyes of those who never knew them, they remain frozen in time.

Appendix

Victims of Sabena Flight 548 who represented the United States Figure Skating Association.

Ann Campbell, 52, Los Angeles. Mother of Roger Campbell and wife of Albert Campbell. She was a former ice dancer who was helping William Kipp coach her son and his partner to their victory in 1961.

Roger Campbell, 18, Arctic Blades Figure Skating Club, Paramount, California. He was the U.S. bronze medalist in ice dance with Yvonne Littlefield in 1960. They placed eighth in the world. He attended the Hollywood Professional School for gifted young athletes, movie stars, and television actors. He won a silver medal in ice dance at the 1961 U.S. Championships with partner Dona Lee Carrier, earning him passage to Prague. He and Dona Lee also finished second at the 1961 North American Championships. He was the only son of Albert and Ann Campbell.

Dona Lee Carrier, 20, Skating Club of Los Angeles. The only child of the Reverend and Mrs. Floyd C. Carrier, she skated in Troy, New York, until the family moved to North Hollywood in 1958, where she took Roger Campbell as a partner in 1960. Dona Lee attended the Hollywood Professional School for gifted young athletes, movie stars, and television actors. She and Roger finished second in ice dance at the 1961 U.S. Nationals, earning her a ticket to Prague. The couple also finished second at the 1961 North American Championships.

Robert and Patricia Dineen, 25 (both), Skating Club of Lake Placid. This husband-and-wife team had won the U.S. silver dance title in 1960, and the Eastern gold dance title in 1961, before winning the bronze medal in ice dance at the 1961 U.S. Nationals. Prague was to be their first appearance at the World Championships. They had an eight-month-old son, Robert, Jr., who was adopted by his uncle after the crash. They were coached by Ronald Ludington, who could not afford the plane ticket to Worlds. They placed sixth at the North American Championships.

Alvah "Linda" Hadley, 33, Seattle. Along with coaching her two children, Ila Ray and Ray Hadley, she helped her husband, Ray, run the Hadley and Hart Skating Studio in Seattle. She skated professionally under the name Linda Hart. Her husband was supposed to join the family in Prague the day after they were to have landed.

Ila Ray Hadley, 18, and Ray Hadley, 17, Seattle Skating Club. This brother-and-sister team finished eleventh at the 1960 Olympics. They won the U.S. junior pairs championship in 1957. They claimed the Pacific Coast senior pairs titles in 1959 and 1960. In 1960, they were the Pacific Coast silver dance champions. In 1961, they won the silver medal at the U.S. National Championships, earning them a place on the World Team. They also placed fourth at the North American Championships.

Harold Hartshorne, 69, and Louisa Hartshorne, 52, Skating Club of New York. Harold Hartshorne was a Princeton graduate and one of the foremost experts in ice dance in the early twentieth century. In the thirties and forties, he competed in fifteen U.S. National Championships, and collected five gold medals along the way. Hartshorne was one of the founders of the Skating Club of

New York, and served as its president until his death. From 1938-1941, Hartshorne served as the United States Figure Skating Association dance committee chairperson. While serving in this post, Hartshorne was instrumental in the development and standardization of the modern international dances. He went on to become a world dance judge, then a world dance referee in 1960. He was scheduled to judge the 1961 World Championships in Prague, and he decided to bring his wife, Louisa, with him so they could enjoy Europe together.

Laurie Jean Hickox, 16, and William Holmes Hickox, 19, Skating Club of San Francisco. Although they represented the Skating Club of San Francisco, this sister-and-brother team trained at the Broadmoor Ice Palace with coach Edi Scholdan, and had been "adopted" as Coloradans by the home crowd. They won the bronze medal at the 1961 U.S. Nationals to earn their very first trip to the World Championships. They placed sixth at the North American Championships. William was an Air Cadet at the U.S. Air Force Academy, and decided to forego an invitation to march in John F. Kennedy's inauguration so he could compete at Nationals with his sister. They were the only children of Lute and Elinor Hickox of Berkeley, California.

Gregory Kelley, 16, Figure Skating Club of Boston, Broadmoor Figure Skating Club. He was the son of Dr. and Mrs. Vincent Kelley and had five siblings. Gregory wanted to be a doctor like his father. He was first inspired to skate after watching Dick Button, and bought a pair of secondhand skates to start. He left the prestigious Figure Skating Club of Boston to skate in Colorado Springs with famous coach Edi Scholdan. He won the U.S. junior title in 1959, and skated at the World Championships in 1960, when the top U.S. skaters withdrew from the competition. He was a member of the

American Numismatic Association and was credited with having the world's largest collection of three-dollar bills. Only sixty-five were known to exist, and Kelley somehow collected forty-two of them. He was second at the U.S. Nationals in 1961, and placed third at the North American Championships. He was also the youngest ever U.S. novice men's champion, winning at age twelve.

Nathalie Kelley, 28, Newton Centre, Massachussetts. Dr. and Mrs. Vincent Kelley sent Nathalie from Boston to Colorado Springs to chaperone her little brother Gregory. She took a leave of absence from her job as a science teacher at Ashland High School to help Gregory realize his dreams. At her parents' request, she boarded the plane to Prague to keep an eye on Gregory. She had also been a competitive skater in her teens. She was the eldest of six children.

William Kipp, Arctic Blades Figure Skating Club. Originally from Allentown, Pennsylvania, he moved to Paramount, California, to coach. His most famous pupil was Peggy Fleming, but she was only competing at the novice level of competition when he was killed on Sabena Flight 548. He was coaching ladies bronze medalist Rhode Michelson, and dancers Roger Campbell and Dona Lee Carrier. Known as "Billy" to his friends and family, he began skating as a child because, as an asthmatic, he could not tolerate outdoor sports. His teacher was Swiss-born Gus Lussi, who also coached Dick Button. Kipp had passed his gold tests in both figures and dance, a rare accomplishment. Just as he seemed headed for the Olympics, he badly twisted his leg, and never regained his form. He turned down a job as a headliner with Ice Follies so he could coach. He was outspoken in his opinion that ice dance should be in the Olympics, a dream that was realized more than twenty years after his death.

Edward LeMaire, 36, Rye, New York. A decorated Navy pilot in World War II, he attended Yale University and graduated from the University of Nevada. An investment broker, he was scheduled to judge at the 1962 Worlds but was asked to go to Prague in 1961 to prepare for the voting pressure often applied by Eastern-block judges. Edward's father had skated in international ice revues, and his mother was a performer with the Reynolds circus family. He skated in an exhibition at the 1932 Olympics at age seven. He won a National junior pairs title in 1942 and a National junior men's title in 1943. LeMaire was also a champion roller skater, who taught himself how to roller skate on a dare. Three weeks after first putting on roller skates, he was a national champion. He and his wife, Muriel, had two daughters and a son.

Richard "Dickie" LeMaire, 13, Rye, New York. He just recovered from a bout with osteomyelitis and was going to Europe with his dad, Edward LeMaire, for the educational value. His great passion was rooting for the Yale football team.

Bradley Lord, 21, Figure Skating Club of Boston. He started skating when he was eleven but never planned to make a career of it. He placed sixth at the World Championships in 1960, as an alternate to the U.S. team. He had missed making the 1960 Olympic team by 94/100ths of a point. His father, Roy "Lefty" Lord, was a designer of high-end ladies shoes for the Copley Shoe Company. His mother, Alfreda, was known to attend every competition. He came back from being second in school figures to win the Nationals in 1961, barely overcoming Gregory Kelley in the standings. He won the silver at the 1961 North American Championships. His mother and his coach Montgomery "Bud" Wilson, were supposed to go to Prague with him but were busy planning the Figure Skating Club of Boston's famous "Ice Chips" show, so they decided to stay home.

Deane E. McMinn, 41, Lomita, California. He was asked to serve as the team manager on the trip to Prague. He was a former skater and a respected judge. McMinn was one of the founding members of the Arctic Blades Figure Skating Club of Paramount, California. He judged at the 1960 Squaw Valley Olympics, and the 1960 North American Championships. McMinn was also responsible for the creation and adoption of pairs tests. McMinn had served on a P.T. boat in the Navy during World War II. He took a leave of absence from his civilian accounting job with the U.S. Coast Guard to attend Worlds.

Rhode Lee Michelson, 17, Arctic Blades Figure Skating Club. She had won the U.S. ladies novice title in 1958, then became the 1959 Pacific Coast ladies champion. She was fifth after the compulsory figures at the 1961 U.S. Nationals but put forth the most difficult free skate of the competition, capturing the bronze medal and a ticket to Prague. She nearly missed the flight to Prague after suffering a hip injury at the North American Championships, which forced her to withdraw from the event.

Laurence Rochon Owen, 16, Figure Skating Club of Boston. U.S. and North American ladies champion in 1961, she was third at U.S. Nationals in 1960, and placed sixth in the Squaw Valley Olympics and ninth at the 1960 World Championships. She aspired to be a writer, like her mother, nine-time U.S. skating champion Maribel Vinson Owen. Her father, Guy Owen, was a former Canadian junior champion. She was also the younger sister of 1961 U.S. pairs champion Maribel Y. Owen. She had earned early admission to Radcliffe.

Maribel Vinson Owen, 49, Figure Skating Club of Boston/ Commonwealth Club. She won her first U.S National title in 1928 and won the next five championships. She won again in 1935. She competed in three Olympics between 1928 and 1936, losing each time to Sonja Henie, the Norwegian queen of skating. Maribel's best showing was in 1932, when she won the bronze medal. She also won five senior pairs titles, with two different partners. She won with Thornton Coolidge in 1928 and 1929, and with George Hill in 1933, 1935, 1936, and 1937. She coached numerous world and Olympic medalists, including the first American woman to win a gold in figure skating, Tenley Albright. She was married to Canadian skater Guy Owen, who died in 1952. She supported her daughters Maribel, Jr. and Laurence by coaching, and by taking writing jobs with the Associated Press. She wrote three instructional books on skating and was the first female sportswriter for the *New York Times*. Her coaching methods are still being used today, through her pupils Frank Carroll and Ron Ludington, who coach some of today's most well-known skaters.

Maribel Yerxa Owen, 20, Figure Skating Club of Boston. She placed sixth at the 1959 World Championships with pairs partner Dudley Richards. A senior at Boston University, majoring in sociology and anthropology, she aspired to be a teacher. She was the daughter of Maribel Vinson Owen and Guy Owen, and the older sister of Laurence Owen. She is credited with convincing the USFSA to change the competitive schedule to one that placed the U.S. Nationals before the World Championships, a rule change that stands to this day. Her friends say she and partner Dudley Richards were planning to wed. They finished first at the 1961 U.S. Nationals and second at the 1961 North American championships.

Dallas "Larry" Pierce, 24, Winter Club of Indianapolis. He placed second in the United States, and fifth in the world in 1960 with partner Marilyn Meeker. They were the 1959 U.S. junior ice dance champions. Pierce had served in the U.S. Marines, and attended Indiana University for two years. When Meeker broke her ankle six weeks before the 1961 U.S. Nationals, he convinced Diane Sherbloom of Los Angeles to move to Indianapolis and train with him. Five weeks later, they were national champions and on their way to Prague. Pierce and Sherbloom finished fourth at the North American Championships.

Walter Powell, 81, Skating Club of St. Louis. A retired executive of the Brown Shoe Company in St. Louis, Powell followed skating throughout his adult life. He served as president of the USFSA from 1943-1946 and was the first U.S. office holder in the International Skating Union (ISU). His standout accomplishment was obtaining separate membership for the U.S. and Canada within the ISU. Powell had served as a referee in both the 1952 Oslo Olympics and the 1960 Squaw Valley Olympics. He also refereed the 1961 U.S. Nationals and was scheduled to be the referee of the Prague Worlds. In his will, Powell left two million dollars to his wife, who donated it to the St. Louis Symphony Orchestra. The performance hall is now named Powell Hall in his honor.

Douglas Ramsay, 16, Detroit Skating Club. Known as "Dick Button, Jr.," Doug was the only man in the 1961 U.S. Nationals to perform a triple jump, and he had the biggest support from the crowd. Due to a poor performance in school figures, Doug only finished fourth. As team alternate, he was issued a ticket on Sabena Flight 548 when the U.S. bronze medalist, Tim Brown, was diagnosed with heart trouble. Doug was famous for barely beating Maribel Vinson Owen's student Frank Carroll in the 1960 junior men's championship. He finished fourth at the 1961 North American Championships and was considered the true show-stealer of the event.

Dudley Shaw Richards, 29, Figure Skating Club of Boston. As of 1961, "Dud" had the longest competitive skating career of anyone, spanning twenty years. He graduated in 1954 with a degree in history from Harvard, where he earned a special "Major H" in non-college sports. He skated pairs with Olympic gold medalist Tenley Albright, but after a practice accident, Tenley's father told her she could not skate pairs anymore. Dud served in the Army, then took Maribel Y. Owen as his partner, all while working in a real estate firm. They placed sixth in the world in 1959, and finished tenth at the 1960 Olympics. They won the gold medal in pairs at the 1961 U.S. Nationals, and placed second at the North American Championships. Friends say he was going to propose marriage to Mara once they arrived in Europe.

Daniel Ryan, 32, Winter Club of Indianapolis. He placed third in pairs at the World Championships in 1952 and 1953 with partner Carol Ann Peters. Together, they were U.S. National Champions. He and his wife, Rose Anne, had five children, one of whom was only two weeks old when Daniel boarded Sabena Flight 548, where he was taking his pupil, Larry Pierce, and Larry's new partner, Diane Sherbloom, to Prague.

Edi Scholdan, 49, Broadmoor Figure Skating Club, Colorado Springs, Colorado. He started skating in his native Austria, before joining ice revues in Europe, and eventually, the United States. He served in the U.S. Army military police, then took a job at the Broadmoor Figure Skating Club, where he coached men's Olympic gold medalists Hayes Alan and David Jenkins. For his sense of humor, and for often juggling on skates, he earned the nickname "the clown prince of Broadmoor." He was coaching Gregory Kelley and Stephanie Westerfeld in 1961, and after the championship, he was going to take his son Jimmy to Austria. Edi also had a seven-year-old daughter named Ruthie.

James Scholdan, 12, Colorado Springs, Colorado. He was the son of Broadmoor Figure Skating Club coach Edi Scholdan, and brother of Ruth Scholdan.

Diane Carol Sherbloom, 18, Los Angeles Figure Skating Club. She had won a silver medal at the U.S. Nationals in 1959 with Roger Campbell, but then found herself without a partner in 1961. She had no plans to attend the 1961 U.S. Nationals, but Larry Pierce called and begged her to skate with him, after his original partner broke her ankle. Dee Dee was hesitant, but then relented and went to Indianapolis. Five weeks later, she and Larry had won the U.S. National Championships in ice dance. They finished fourth at the North American Championships.

William Swallender, 52, Detroit Figure Skating Club. Swallender was a former senior men's Midwestern champion and went on to skate with the Ice Follies. He was the first coach at the Kansas City Skating Club. He also coached in Baltimore, Chicago, and eventually, Detroit. His student, Doug Ramsay, finished fourth at the 1961 U.S. Nationals and was not invited to Prague. When bronze medalist Tim Brown dropped out due to heart trouble, Ramsay and Swallender were issued tickets aboard Sabena Flight 548.

Sharon Westerfeld, 25, Broadmoor Figure Skating Club. She was an alternate to the 1955 U.S. World team, but then she quit amateur skating. After graduating from Colorado College with a degree in psychology, she worked at a jewelry store to help finance her little sister's skating lessons. She went to Prague to chaperone Stephanie, when she made the 1961 World Team.

Stephanie Westerfeld, 17, Broadmoor Figure Skating Club. An accomplished pianist, honor student, ballroom dancer, and homecoming queen at Cheyenne Mountain High School, she narrowly missed earning a place on the Olympic team in 1960. Steffi finished second at the 1961 U.S. Nationals and was fourth at the 1961 North American Championships. She was invited to participate in a national piano competition during the same week of Nationals, but ultimately chose to skate instead.

Other Passengers Aboard Sabena Flight 548

Julian Baginski, Englewood Cliffs, New Jersey
Pierre Balteau, Stamford, Connecticut
Germaine Berbruggen, Brussels, Belgium
Jean Berbruggen, Brussels, Belgium
Father Otmar Boesch, Seattle, Washington
Alexander Dayton, Olney, Texas
Marcellin Deprince, De Panne, Belgium
Iris Duke, Dallas, Texas
Linda Foster, Houston, Texas
Dorice Herring, Dallas, Texas
Maurice Herring, Dallas, Texas
Jacob Herschkowicz, Jackson Heights, New York
Harold Kellett, Bronxville, New York
Juanita Lemoine, New Orleans, Louisiana
Howard Lillie, Corning, New York
Vanessa Maes, Ontario, Canada
Victor Maes, Ontario, Canada
Francisco Medina, Winnetka, Illinois
Herbert Myers, East Orange, New Jersey
Franz Offergelt, Hansent, Belgium
Margaret Pozzuolo, Drexel Hill, Pennsylvania
Jacqueline Robinson, Winona Lake, Indiana
Richard Robinson, U.S. Armed Forces
Robert Raulier, Brussels, Belgium

Max Silberstein, Westport, Connecticut
Martin Soria, East Lansing, Michigan
Private First Class Robert Stopp, U.S. Armed Forces
Dominique Vernier, Mouscron, Belgium
George Young, Olney, Texas

Crew Aboard Sabena Flight 548

Pierre van den Busche, Steward
Marcel DeMayer, Steward
Lucien Eduwaere, Flight Engineer
Paul Evos, Steward
Jean Kint, Navigator
Louis Lambrechts, Captain
Jacqueline Rombaut, Hostess
Jean Roy, Co-captain
Jacqueline Trullemans, Hostess
Henri Vernimmen, Steward
Robert Voleppe, Steward

Much of the research for this work involved lengthy interviews with dozens of family members, friends, competitors, and students of the victims of Sabena Flight 548. Those interviewed are among some of the elite members of the skating world. Former world champions, Olympic medalists, and former USFS presidents are among those who granted interviews to the author. The World Figure Skating Museum and Hall of Fame set up many of these interviews on behalf of the author through a paid research assistance service.

The archives of the World Figure Skating Museum and Hall of Fame provided numerous press clippings stored at the museum. We are unable to list the names of all publications, as the clippings stored in the museum did not always reveal the publication name. Also in the museum archives, the author found dozens of letters between the association and family members, condolence messages, essays about the victims, and hall of fame displays outlining the contributions of those who perished. The *CBS Sports Spectacular* broadcast tape of the 1961 Nationals was especially helpful in painting vivid portraits of the skaters.

As with any historical event, memories do fade. Facts are blurred or misremembered. Sometimes sources contradicted each other, either on points of fact or in their opinions about people and events. In these cases, I relied on journalistic judgment, using two or more sources to confirm a point and either noting in the text a discrepancy among sources or presenting the majority's opinion. Therefore, the story as I've presented it is based on judgments I have made as the author and does not necessarily reflect the view of all the people listed as sources.

Chapter 1

Skating Magazine, March 1961.

CBS Sports Spectacular, January, 1961.

Harvard Varsity Club News and Views, "Figure Skating and Harvard ... A Perfect Pair: Many Crimson Skaters Have Made Their Way to the Olympic Podium," John Powers, Volume 46, 2004.

Houston Chronicle, "Greatest Miracle Never Told," Mickey Herskowitz, February 7, 2004.

Chapter 2

The Fun of Figure Skating, A Primer of the Art, Maribel Vinson Owen, Harper and Row Publishers, 1960.

Boston Globe, Bob, Duffy, "Remembering Flight 548, Shattered Dreams," December 29, 2000.

Kansas City Star, "Frozen in Time: 40 Years After Plane Crash, Figure Skaters Are Remembered," Mechelle Voepel, March 3, 2001.

Chapter 3

CBS Sports Spectacular, January, 1961.

Skating Magazine, March 1961.

Colorado Springs Gazette, "US Skating Tragedy: Plane Crash Resonates in Springs and Beyond," Kamon Simpson, February 2001.

Kansas City Star, "The Legacy," Bill Norton, date unknown.

Chapter 4

The Story of Figure Skating, Michael Boo, Morrow Junior Books, 1999.

Queen of Ice, Queen of Shadows: The Unsuspected Life of Sonja Henie, Raymond Strait, Leif Henie, Stein and Day, 1985.

The New York Times, "Maribel Vinson Owen," Arthur Daley, February 16, 1961.

United States Olympic Committee, Official Report on the 1932 Lake Placid Olympic Games.

Ottawa Citizen, April 21, 1952.

Associate Press Wire, Sport Editor Ted Smits' reflections on Owen Skating Family, February 1961.

Newsweek, "The Bright Hope Killed," February 27, 1961.

Chapter 5

Skating Magazine, March 1961.

CBS Sports Spectacular, January, 1961.

USA Today, "Cohen Not Afraid to Mix it Up During Warmups," Christine Brennan, January 16, 2002.

Chapter 6

CBS Sports Spectacular, January, 1961.

Skating Magazine, March 1961

Skating History Lesson: Hollywood Professional School, Jo Ann Schneider Farris.

Chapter 7

Skating Abroad on 44 Pounds, David Jenkins.

Around the World on Pounds, Carol Heiss.

Final Crash Report, Sabena Flight 548, Belgian Ministry of Communications.

Boston Globe, "Mrs. Owen Championed Cause of Young Skaters", Ed Costello, February 15, 1961.

Kansas City Star, "The Legacy," Bill Norton, date unknown.

Chapter 8

Rene J. Francillon, *Boeing 707: Pioneer Jetliner,* MBI Publishing Company, 1999.

New York Times, Arthur Daley, February 16, 1961.

Turbulent Skies: The History of Commercial Aviation, T.A. Heppenheimer, John Wiley and Sons, 1998.

Final Crash Report, Sabena Flight 548, Belgian Ministry of Communications.

Kansas City Star, "The Legacy," Bill Norton, date unknown.

Chapter 9

Sports Illustrated, "Mother Sets the Style: Laurence Owen is America's Most Exciting Girl Skater, but at Home, She's Just Another Champion," Barbara Heilman, February 13, 1961.

Seattle Times, February 15, 1961.

Los Angeles Mirror, February 15, 1961.

Los Angeles Times, February 15, 1961.

Chapter 10

Final Crash Report, Sabena Flight 548, Belgian Ministry of Communications.

Sports Illustrated, "Mother Sets the Style: Laurence Owen is America's Most Exciting Girl Skater, but at Home, She's Just Another Champion," Barbara Heilman, February 13, 1961.

Rene J. Francillon, *Boeing 707: Pioneer Jetliner,* MBI Publishing Company, 1999.

Chapter 11

Time Magazine, *A Family Affair,* February 24, 1961.

Newsweek, *The Bright Hope Killed,* February 27, 1961.

Chapter 12

Allentown Morning Call, February 15, 1961.

The Long Program, Skating Toward Life's Victories, Peggy Fleming, Pocket Books, 1999.

Sports Illustrated, "40 for the Ages," September 19, 1994.

Boston Globe, "No Routine Event," John Powers, January 17, 2001.

Recommended Reading

Frozen Assets: The New Order of Figure Skating, Mark Lund, Rebecca Patrick, Lloyd Elfman, Ashton International Media, Inc., 2003

The Long Program: Skating Toward Life's Victories, Peggy Fleming, Pocket Books, 2000.

The Complete Book of Figure Skating, Carole Shulman and Donald Laws, Human Kinetics, December 2001.

The author wishes to thank those individuals who took part in interviews or who sent comments via e-mail:

Roberto Agnolini
Dr. Tenley Albright
William Boeck
Jim Browning
Joyce Butchart
Dr. Lorraine Hanlon Comanor
Debbie Conrad
William Cunningham
Howard Deardorff
Annie and Diane de Leeuw
Susan Duncan
Jane Dystel
Charles Foster
Dan Hollander
Eileen Seigh Honnen
Don Jackson
Maria Jelinek
Jane Bucher Jones
U.S. Senator Edward M. Kennedy
Sally Knoll
Tonia Kwiatkowski
Sandy Lamb
Ron Ludington
Mickey Leiter
Paul Maca
Virginia Might
Mark Mitchell
John Nicks
Roberta Parkinson
Diane Yeomans Robins
Elizabeth (Sherry) Ruch
Allison Scott
Cathy Stevensen
Tom Schiebel
Diana LeMaire Squibb
Elizabeth Viken
Rose Anne Wager
Ben and Mary Louise Wright

Index

About the Author

Nikki Nichols is a journalist and a competitive figure skater. As a journalist, she has worked at four television stations around the United States. Her writing has appeared in *Skating Magazine*, the *Indianapolis Star*, *Indianapolis Prime Times*, and numerous trade journals and Web sites. She has been featured in the *Indianapolis Business Journal*.

As a skater, she has won an Indiana state title, a sectional title in the adults age 25-35 division, and was a finalist at the 2005 U.S. Adult National Championships. Nikki is a 1997 cum laude graduate of Butler University. She currently works as public relations and marketing manager for the National Committee on Planned Giving in Indianapolis. Nikki is engaged to be married to her pairs partner, Michael J. Cunningham. They will reside in Indianapolis.

Memorial Fund

Securing our future by remembering our past

Established on February 23, 1961, the mission of the Memorial Fund is twofold: to honor the 1961 World Figure Skating Team and to provide qualified skaters with financial assistance to pursue their goals both inside and outside the competitive arena.

The Memorial Fund is committed to awarding athletic and academic grants and scholarships to athletes who have demonstrated outstanding competitive results and/or academic achievements and exhibit potential for excellence in national and international competition.

Having distributed more than $3.8 million since 1993, the Memorial Fund currently awards $350,000 annually to qualified skaters via the Competitive Skaters Assistance Program and the Academic Scholarship Program.

To learn more, or to make a donation to the Memorial Fund, please visit www.usfigureskating.org.